I've travelled the world twice over,
Met the famous: saints and sinners,
Poets and artists, kings and queens,
Old stars and hopeful beginners,
I've been where no-one's been before,
Learned secrets from writers and cooks
All with one library ticket
To the wonderful world of books.

© JANICE JAMES.

TRIUMPH OVER DARKNESS

Born in France in 1809, Louis Braille was the fourth child of a village saddler. At the age of three, he stabbed himself in the eye with a pointed tool from his father's bench. Some thirteen years later he used a similar sharp tool to create a code of raised dots punched through sheets of paper. With patience he perfected his code and fashioned an alphabet that opened the world of learning for the blind. Louis Braille died at the age of forty-three unknown and unhonoured.

LENNARD BICKEL

TRIUMPH OVER DARKNESS

The life of Louis Braille

Complete and Unabridged

ULVERSCROFT
Leicester

First published in Australia in 1988 by
Allen and Unwin Australia Pty. Ltd.,
Sydney

First Large Print Edition
published June 1989

British Library CIP Data

Bickel, Lennard
    Triumph over darkness.—Large print ed.—
Ulverscroft large print series: non-fiction
I. Title
362.4'1'0924

ISBN 0-7089-2004-7

Published by
F. A. Thorpe (Publishing) Ltd.
Anstey, Leicestershire
Set by Rowland Phototypesetting Ltd.
Bury St. Edmunds, Suffolk
Printed and bound in Great Britain by
T. J. Press (Padstow) Ltd., Padstow, Cornwall

For
Jan Smark Nilsson

Tribute

IT is high time for Louis Braille's genius to be recognised throughout the earth and for the story to be told of the godlike courage and the heart of gold with which he built a large, firm stairway for millions of sense-crippled human beings to climb, from hopeless darkness to the Mind Eternal.

Were it not for Louis Braille, the world of the blind would be quite drab, worse than it would be for the seeing without ink-print books. Out of personal experience I give deepest thanks to Louis Braille, who dropped upon the Sahara of blindness his gift of inexhaustible fertility and joy. I studied at Radcliffe College (USA) with the aid of European Braille books, not only in English, but also in French, German and Greek. The world around me shone afresh with treasures of poetry, and thought on philosophy, history and literature in other lands. Enraptured, I sensed my membership of the human race anew.

Louis Braille died a complete human being, though blind; great because he greatly used his loss of sight to liberate his afflicted fellow creatures. The unwearied activity of his clear, scientific mind, his calmness and forbearance, his inventive abilities as a teacher, the wealth of his heart expended in uncounted secret gifts out of scant savings to the needy—both blind and seeing—are a priceless legacy.

Helen Keller—1952
(On the centenary of the death
of Louis Braille.
By courtesy of the Royal National
Institute for the Blind, London.)

Access to communication in the widest sense is access to knowledge, and that is vitally important for us if we are not to go on being despised or patronised by condescending sighted people. We do not need pity, nor do we need to be reminded that we are vulnerable. We must be treated as equals—and communication is the way we can bring this about.

Louis Braille
1841

1

The First Step

THE decades of bloodshed that stained the end of the eighteenth century in France made the capital, Paris, an unlikely birthplace for historic advance in the human condition. Then a tawdry, crowded city, and the most populous in Europe, Paris daily witnessed poverty, misery, cold and hunger on a shocking scale. Suffering was taken as a mode of life and met with an indifference that was as cruel as the imperial dictatorship that would follow.

It was still the seat—by divine right—of the Bourbons, supreme rulers of the *ancien régime*, who seemed destined never to learn, never to scent the wind of change, unable to see doom breeding in the squalid streets and alleyways of crowded tenements not a stone's throw from the back doors of their splendid residences and palaces. In blissful oblivion

1

they were uncaring of suffering and of the simmering anger, rising to hatred, that would soon convulse both city and nation in the blood-lust of vengeful revolution. Apathy, heartless lack of concern and indifference to affliction were national traits at this time. Life was cheap to princes of the blood and *la noblesse*, as cheap as it would be to the ghouls of the Reign of Terror and to the ambitious First Consul, who would later crown himself Emperor and be seen riding the corpse-littered battlefield of Borodino bouncing with glee in the saddle when counting five dead Russians for every slain Frenchman.

In the eighth decade of the century the gulf between privileged possession and the poor and handicapped was ominously wide. Paris—so different to the modern metropolis—was hemmed about with medieval fortifications, such as the old Bastille, studded with palaces and gothic churches and splendid abbeys, while solid mansions lined the famous boulevards, the faubourgs of St-Honoré, St-Marceau, St-Jacques and St-Germain, fringed by the green belts of the Champs-Elysées and Champ de Mars, still then open country.

Caught within all this, behind the facades of ornate homes occupied by elegant gentlefolk, some 600,000 people huddled into hovels sandwiched in rabbit warrens of tangled streets and narrow winding alleyways. This multitude of hungry, impoverished people existed among squalor and filth, where night-pots and wastes were emptied into the gutters, where the only light that shone came from the sky, where the only water used came from some public fountain or the bank of the polluted river; where, consequently, disease was rampant among young and old alike. And in those years, so critical to European and world history, nature added its barbs to the suffering. Winters were so savage the river froze, and there were shortages, not only of food, but also of fuel for heating; while summers seemed to come with fierce apology, the sun baking the land into submission and ruining harvests that might have brought relief.

And still the royal circus continued on its frivolous path, with no other government for the nation; the nobility and wealthy landholders maintained their graceful way of life, blithely indifferent to the rage that would end their privilege in a tide of blood, with pillaging of fine homes, desecration of churches and the murder of priests and raping of nuns.

Such was the backdrop in early autumn of 1771, when a young Frenchman met with an experience that moved him so deeply that he was committed to a mission that, eventually, would reach out to touch the lives of millions yet to be born. In that year, after the heat of summer had lifted from Paris, the fashionable life of the city was returning to activity; the well-to-do came back from summer retreats to their ornate mansions, fine carriages drawn by teams of high-stepping percherons were again rolling along the boulevards—and the Sunday parades were resumed. The paths of favourite parks, such as Ruggieri's or the more sedate Tuileries (which had been created for Catherine of Medici two centuries earlier), were scenes of colour, where women in full skirts, dainty frilled blouses and wide bonnets strolled with gentlemen, dandies in bright high-collared coats, ribboned perukes under tricorne hats, white hose and buckled shoes and slim rapiers swinging from silvered belts,

4

all of them nodding and smiling faintly at passing acquaintances.

This was formality, families strolling together, to be seen by others in their finest clothes, to be seen to be well-to-do. For younger men there were other attractions on an autumn Sunday. There were the traditional fairs of Paris, noisy, brash, challenging gatherings that competed with the sedate parades. And on this second Sunday in September 1771, there was the Foire St-Ovide, within sight and sound of the sedate processions in the Tuileries, close enough to attract a serious young man in his mid-twenties from an ambling group.

M. Valentin Haüy had but a little way to walk from the riverside park to the Place Louis Grande, later the Place Vendôme. Scion of a middle-class family of weavers in the Picardy town of St-Just, he was, at twenty-five years of age, a skilled interpreter in the Ministry of Foreign Affairs and younger brother to a noted cleric and scientist, Abbé René-Just Haüy (then about to found the study of crystallography). Valentin Haüy was an upright young man of noble brow, calm grey eyes, generous mouth, chin firm above his lace cravat. Like many others that Sunday, he was drawn into the vibrant throng at the boisterous fair.

Long before this day the Foire St-Ovide had left behind its original purpose of honouring a little-remembered saint. It now had a character of its own; it was part of the autumnal scene of Paris, with the special attraction of its *pain d'épice*, a hot, spiced honey-bread that appealed to Parisian taste-buds and drew a motley crowd. The Foire St-Ovide was a world within a world, where the well-born and well-dressed would rub shoulders with *hoi polloi*, where young blades and swaggering soldiers, with wide moustaches and long swords, would seek the girls with rouged cheeks and low-cut dresses, where idlers, beggars, and pickpockets moved through the throng, everybody stepping carefully over muddy puddles and animal droppings, all being loudly invited to the showings of quacks and mountebanks with cures for every known ailment, being cajoled by buskers for sideshows to see a lamb with two heads, or a man with no arms; and by pedlars with displays of baubles and ornaments, some ringing bells, some seeking attention by banging tambourines, others with whistles or horns. And above all this jangle were the sounds from the open-air cafés and the covered cabaret-taverns.

M. Valentin Haüy sought his serving of hot, spiced honey-bread at a cabaret-tavern noisier than the others, because there he could have a table close to the stage. There he could gaze into the faces of the performers, a group of garishly garbed men and youths whose actions were arousing gales of derisive laughter from the audience. M. Haüy had come to the moment that would give meaning to his life, and inspire a selfless dedication that would put his life at risk but would virtually go unrecognised by the French nation. The group of performers were all blind, a make-believe orchestra under the baton of a conductor who was also without sight.

In the late eighteenth century the plight of sightless people was widely known and commonly accepted. Along with people of his class and time, Valentin Haüy was accustomed to blind people begging in the city streets. On the highways it was common to find groups of sightless people —men, women and children—drifting wretchedly and hopelessly from place to place, often harried, usually ignored, generally avoided or repulsed for their ungainly, shuffling gait, their ragged dirty appearance, for their talon-like hands held out in endless cadging and pleading for scraps of food. Whether on the highways or huddled in some corner of the cold city, these people were regarded as incomplete beings, ignorant and simple. There had been a few individual acts of charity. In France in the thirteenth century the Crusader King, Louis XI, had set up a hospice for aged blind derelicts. Known as the Quinze-Vingt asylum, it was no more than a place for the old blind to die, and over the years it had become marred by squalor and neglect. Little was done to change the common attitude, and humiliation and indignity was shown to the blind on all sides. Where blind people were given work, it was menial; and young, sightless boys and girls were often sold to chimney sweeps, who thrust them like human brushes into blocked flues. Sightless adults were put into rings in travelling circuses to fight as blind gladiators to amuse customers.

A few blind people had made their mark over time, people with outstanding character and ability to lift them above a useless mendicant life. There had been a musician or two, a philosopher or a singer, but these were islands in an ocean of unconcern. These more fortunate blind were usually people with the advantages of money and family.

In the general view, blindness was punishment for sin against God; and this intolerance often led to vicious reprisal. The mould of public rejection remained uncracked, and blind people had yet, in the words of the remarkable Helen Keller, "to emerge from the degradation that had pursued them down the ages".

Not until Valentin Haüy sat to eat his spiced honey-bread on an autumn Sunday in 1771 at a table in the crowded noisy Foire St-Ovide in Paris had any effective attempt been born to change the common attitude of unconcern.

The young Frenchman never did eat his simple repast. As he sat at the rough wooden table, his gaze transfixed on the performers on the platform, deep compassion welled his heart. He was appalled, repulsed. A dozen blind men and youths were dressed as idiots, in outrageously silly gowns with frills, dunces' caps on their heads and cut-out cardboard spectacles glued to their noses. Paraded as mock musicians, with vacant expressions on their sightless faces, without pretence at harmony, they went through the motions of scraping at violins, cellos, double basses, without a trace of skill, producing a screeching cacophony of discords, immune to the distortion, as though they were deaf or totally devoid of feeling.

The crowded tavern was in an uproar of laughter. Half-drunken men and women yelled abuse and derision and hurled ribald jokes at the blind players; and the more the sightless performers scraped and scratched, the more the audience guffawed and shouted abuse. To Valentin Haüy the entertainment was an obscenity, the treatment of the blind was disgusting. These were handicapped human beings made into blind buffoons, ridiculed and humiliated. For what? A bowl of soup, a crust of bread? Or a few sou? Repelled by the taunts and insults hurled at the unfortunate players, he left the tavern and walked away from the fair. He carried with him a loathing for the callousness in the heart-sickening scene that would last his lifetime. His mind seethed with indignation. Bigots could claim these blind souls were victims of divine wrath, but to Valentin Haüy they were unfortunate people, each and every one a human being afflicted with the loss of the most precious of the senses. It was cruel to mock affliction—it was inhuman and callous.

The impact of his experience at the Foire St-Ovide, the pity and sympathy it aroused on that autumn Sunday in 1771 were branded in his memory. These impressions were still vivid in his mind when he had an unexpected encounter later that same year.

For the gentlefolk of Paris, attending church on Sundays was more a social ritual than an act of devotion and obeisance. To be seen at the cathedral or fashionable church was as important to social standing as it was to be well dressed. One part of the ritual was to give alms on leaving the service. With dignity and hauteur, a few sous would be placed in the hands of a beggar on the steps, customarily the same one each Sunday. And while this donation of the mite could ease conscience, it was also part of a beggar's expected income, so that a place on church steps on Sunday held a right of ownership, claimed by the indigent as though it were property.

Valentin Haüy usually attended the Church of St-Roch, and on a cold, grey November Sunday in 1771 he placed the usual few sou in the hands of the usual beggar and walked on down the street to the meeting that would change his life.

A few yards from the church he came on the boy. The young lad was no more than a bundle of rags, bare-footed, squatting on the pavement against the church wall. Thin, wan with cold, trembling, his two hands were held up in supplication as he heard footsteps approaching. His head was turned towards the cloudy sky, but he saw nothing; his eyes were sightless, his face a blank; and the sympathy and pity that had so moved Valentin Haüy at the autumn fair surged anew. He found a few coins in his purse and placed them, silent, in the outstretched hands, and then watched, suddenly engrossed and fascinated by the boy's fingers. The embossed faces of the coins were explored with delicate touch, fingertips traced the rims for serrations that would indicate higher value. The movements were light, but certain and quick. Valentin Haüy was entranced, not just by the dexterity of the boy's fingers; there was more to this than sorting coins into values by feel. *This was intelligence by touch!* Fingers served as this boy's eyes; their sensitivity carried messages to the brain—and that realisation brought a surge of exaltation. *Intelligence by touch!* And his generous mind was questing: surely, surely, fingers that could reveal the value of coins could also deliver knowledge and understanding to the dark of the mind.

The thought brought inspiration and impulse to innovation that was compelling. Fingers that could detect the value of coins could read the meaning of words, *provided the letters were raised, lifted into relief as were the faces of the embossed coins*. This blind boy could be taught to read, to learn, to acquire by touch the education and knowledge long denied those who could not see.

Standing on the Paris pavement that November day, his cloak wrapped about him against the chill wind, he vowed to break the chains binding the boy to ignorance. With the memory of indignity and humiliation that had been heaped on the blind musicians at the fair still clear in his mind, he decided to make a personal stand against age-old indifference. And this beggar boy would be his first step—"*le premier pas*"—in that campaign.

Haüy rested his hand on the boy's head in a kindly gesture. "How are you called, *garçon*?"

"François, monsieur."

"No other name?"

"Oui, monsieur. Lesueur, François Lesueur."

That moment made a cameo of compassion that would become historic: the cultured, humane, young Frenchman in the role of patron and protector and the ragged blind boy seated at his feet. Now, more than two centuries later, their figures, sculpted in stone, stand at the side of traffic congestion in the Boulevard des

14

Invalides, as little noticed by hurrying Parisians as was the man and his work during the years of dedication. That statue, however, is more than a symbol for Paris: it has world value. It is a token to an act of compassion that was forerunner to similar acts in other lands. Valentin Haüy's statue (along with that of his protégé, François) stands in the grounds of the modern home of the pioneer institution he was to establish, the first of its kind in history.

To admirers, Haüy is known as "Apostle to the Blind", yet his statue represents many who followed him.

It could, for example, be the figure of the American pioneer, Dr. Samuel Gridley Howe (whose wife, Julia Ward Howe, wrote the text to the Battle Hymn of the Republic). Dr. Howe's work, based on the Valentin Haüy model, led to education of such remarkable women as Helen Keller and her "Teacher", Anne Sullivan Macey. The black-bearded humanitarian with the burning eyes of a zealot had fought with Lord Byron for Greek independence, and in his own country's War of Independence, side by side with the Marquis de

Lafayette. Later he had taken in charge, just as Haüy did François Lesueur, a girl named Laura Bridgman. In the newly established Perkins School for the Blind, in Boston, which Dr. Howe headed, Laura was the first known blind-mute to be educated. Dr. Howe visited the Paris institution to study Haüy's methods, and to recruit two teachers of the blind, but in those dank corridors missed the true genius this early work would produce.

From that Sunday in Paris, in November 1771, many other events were to spring, but few were as far-reaching as Valentin Haüy's original inspiration of teaching with raised letters. No claim has been made that he was directly instrumental in bringing emancipation to all the world's blind people, yet he opened a new age of compassion. He lit the lamp with François Lesueur and showed others the way. On that day, when he pledged shelter and education to the beggar boy, he ceased to be Valentin Haüy, civil servant, and became a benefactor destined to win a place among those who alleviate human degradation and the misery of ignorance.

Haüy's first step was to commission a

wood carver to shape a set of little blocks on which the letters of the alphabet and the numerals zero to nine were raised in relief, stylised and enlarged for easy recognition by touch. These were the first tools by which he began the education of the blind, simple wooden blocks that would open the world's knowledge to millions of sightless people.

Literacy could not come quickly to François Lesueur. There had been no pre-conditioning by vision to help him understand the principles of written language. His years had been spent in dark poverty, with no experience of alphabet, words, sentences, other than in sound. Thus Valentin Haüy, in his first task as teacher, faced a daunting challenge to his patience and persistence—and to his dedication. And for the blind boy, also, the demand for application would be just as testing, so that the tutor had to add reward to encouragement; François was paid a few sou each day, equivalent to what he might have collected in begging on the streets.

Valentin Haüy vacated his civil service post. Then, day after day, week after week, he became a constant companion to

François, endlessly placing the boy's fingertips on the little wooden blocks, repeating and repeating the sound of each letter, on and on as the weeks went by, over and over until the nerves would be stretched to breaking-point. It was slow work, torturously slow. Yet, it was the beginning.

Through the long days of winter, into the heat of summer, Valentin Haüy pursued his task, until the day of first delight, when the blind François could put eight fingers on a line of blocks—and spell out his own name. From then on, awakening seemed to flourish in the lad's mind: his finger-reading became more certain, his touch grew more sensitive and rapid. But M. Haüy, in the flush of success, found himself at an impasse. The young Frenchman faced the problem of limitation of simple wooden blocks under the reading fingers; those crude aids could not begin to offer even the most basic educational subjects: geography, grammar, history, arithmetic. The predicament was clear: the solution was an inspiration. His blind pupil had to be given access to books of study as were normal-sighted pupils, but his books would have to be different, the letters would have to be embossed, lifted into relief as on the wood alphabet, to be *read with fingers instead of eyes!*

Books with raised type, no matter how simple the subject-matter, involved a new approach to printing. Having reversed letters pressed through from one side of the paper to the other would mean using heavier paper with a text on one side of the sheet, instead of the normal two sides. The volumes would contain less, and thus would have to be duplicated; as well, the whole process would be fearfully costly. Valentin Haüy faced a dilemma. How could such a production be justified for one single blind boy? The solution opened a glowing concept. If such textbooks and teaching manuals were produced, they could be used many times by many students. And were there not thousands of children in France who could not see? With such books he could offer tuition to at least a few, a dozen, a hundred! Such books could present wonderful vistas to the minds of blind children, and give them confidence to face life.

The prospect was a beckoning horizon

to the young Frenchman. He needed accommodation, support of gifts and donations; and he needed to select blinded juveniles who were as naturally intelligent as François. He gave his life and all he possessed to the project. He travelled to find and talk with blind youngsters, he organised support from family and friends; and his brother, the Abbé Haüy, was a tower of strength, not only in extracting subscriptions from wealthy connections, but in obtaining occupation of a narrow-fronted old house on the Rue Notre-Dame des Victoires.

This building became the home of the first school in the world for blind juveniles; and one of the first blind teachers in this establishment was the former beggar boy, François Lesueur. Four years from the day Valentin Haüy had sat appalled at the derision heaped on blind musicians in the tavern at Foire St-Ovide, his pupils began to acquire their knowledge of written language, passing through the same initiation as François Lesueur had done in simple subjects—spelling, grammar, history and geography—by finger-reading the dozen original books with the typescript lifted into relief, and cards outlined with shapes of countries and continents. In the world's first classroom for blind children, pupils were avid for learning that would bestow dignity.

Valentin Haüy's distinctive philanthropy soon won attention. The Academy of Literature became interested, and he received an invitation from the eminent Academy of Sciences to lecture to that august body on his methods, and took some of his pupils to demonstrate their learning. When this was done, the savants of France were so impressed that they asked M. Haüy to supply them with regular reports on his progress.

This event proved to be a pebble dropped into a pool of influence; the ripples reached into the elegant circles of the Palace of Versailles.

King Louis XVI and his Queen were given to light *divertissement*. The King was a mild man, who had more interest in tinkering with his collection of watches and clocks than the national economy; Marie Antoinette—daughter of the formidable Empress Maria Theresa of Austria—was said to be extravagant and frivolous.

Against the usual court boredom of the *nuit de Noël* in 1786, the idea of a Christmas demonstration and reading by pupils of the school for blind juveniles seemed appealing. By royal command, M. Valentin Haüy took a group of his children to the ornate surroundings of Versailles, where they were paraded before the King and Queen and an audience of nobles and their ladies.

In records of that time, which survived the trauma of the coming years, historians found evidence that Marie Antoinette took delight in testing whether the students were actually reading with their fingers or just intoning from memory; she had tests made by nobles to prove that the exhibition was genuine, and she herself selected a poem in one of the embossed books to be finger-read. In that light-hearted atmosphere, at Christmas 1786, was the bestowing of the impressive title —Institut *Royale* des Jeunes Aveugles— and promise of the bending of the royal ear should help be needed in the future.

It was a kingly gesture; but it would bring peril to the founder and neglect in the future years of the institute. Time was running out for the easy days of divine right under the *ancien régime*. Two ominous Christmases lay ahead, straddled by winters of savage cold, failed harvests, with resulting famines of food and fuel for workers in town and country. And France was bankrupt.

There would be no royal ducats for the pupils of Valentin Haüy's school for the young blind. The king, desperate to fill his coffers so as to sustain his prodigal way of life, called together the Estates-General—the only form of common government France had known—which had not met for more than a century! The regal request for more money was put to this gathering of noblemen, wealthy land-owners and high-ranking clergy. King Louis blithely expected an agreement to impose new taxes across the country; but the "Third Estate", of land-owners and merchants, had other ideas, and they inflicted the first dent in the monolith of the monarchy. They demanded a limit to customary regal powers and more direct government. They declared the Estates-General to be a National Assembly, and they told the King

23

that "this Assembly will not accept royal orders".

The National Assembly could not give crucial orders; it could not supply bread and fuel for the famished, cold people. By April 1789 empty stomachs fed furious anger; defiant mobs roamed the streets of Paris. There was burning and pillaging. Royal tombs in the ancient St-Antoine were desecrated and relics thrown into the streets. The military fired, Frenchmen died, and blood spilled on the cobbles was to swell into a river. In July an arsenal was broken into and the mob stormed the Bastille, released six prisoners (including the infamous Marquis de Sade), decapitated the governor and his assistant, and carried their heads on poles through the streets.

The tide of terror spread from the city through the countryside, bringing to the many country mansions what Thomas Jefferson—then America's plenipotentiary to France—noted as *la grande peur*. It was indeed great fear, justified by subsequent horrors of bloody retribution in the Place de la Révolution, which preceded the rise of the egotistical

Emperor and a decade of warfare that literally shook the Western world and brought disaster to the world's first school for blind juveniles.

From 1790 onwards, with the ruling Convention swayed by vindictive orators—such as Robespierre and Georges Danton—demanding royal blood, there was no room for compassion, no thought for blind juveniles or their plight. Indeed, the "royal" appellation seemed to earn short shrift for the sightless youngsters. Without ceremony they were plucked from the care of Valentin Haüy and dumped in an asylum for deaf and dumb children and allotted no more tuition than was given to unfortunate mutes. A decade later, Napoleon Bonaparte—as First Consul—condemned the blind youngsters to incarceration in the deplorable Quinze-Vingt workhouse, there to spend years among senile, derelict blind men and women, with the attendant horrors of idleness and neglect.

In the post-revolutionary turmoil, Valentin Haüy was a lone figure imperilled by fateful events. He was one of those people of the so-called Age of Enlightment who—despite the upheaval—were to shape social mores in what historian Albert Cobban would term "the nursery of the modern world". Yet, as the new century unfolded with imperial adventures and social repression, the work of this benefactor of the blind seemed to have passed the peak years, and with his subjects fused into the squalor of the Quinze-Vingt hospice, heartbreak, despair —and danger—were apparent.

The era of the Consulate came with Napoleon Bonaparte drafting his civil code, and the new century was only half a dozen years old when danger became imminent for Valentin Haüy. In the euphoria of Austerlitz and the subjugation of Austria, known sympathisers with the *ancien régime*, people who regarded the Corsican as "The Usurper", were being sought by the *sans culottes*, bands of murderous thugs in striped trousers, whose crimes went unpunished and unrestrained. They sought enemies of the new rule among the so-called "Ultras", among writers and poets, wealthy families, priests and dignitaries of the church.

Early in 1806 Valentin Haüy received

alarming intelligence: the *sans culottes* had turned their attention to his family. His brother, cleric and scientist Abbé René-Just Haüy, had been thrown into prison, in a building on St-Victor that had been an old seminary, and which, by strange fate, would emerge again in the story of Valentin Haüy's school for the blind.

In danger of arrest, Valentin Haüy decided to flee France. In these years of heartache, with the good work he had begun so ruthlessly crushed, and the blind youngsters so heartlessly treated, he had managed to keep contact with some of his former pupils; and one especially held his affection and admiration, Remi Fournier, whose talent for mechanics and whose inventive bent would later play a role in the cause of the blind. Valentin Haüy plucked this youth from the Quinze-Vingt horror, and together they left Paris at night in a closed carriage, on their way to safety in Prussia.

Through the dark hours they rolled eastward from the city of peril, through the parish of Lagny in the shire of Meaux, travelling a roadway a few kilometres from a village tucked into a hillside of the Brie country from which would come the child whose genius would crown the compassion and sacrifice Valentin Haüy had given to his mission.

Eastward the carriage took the founder and his protégé; day and night they drove towards the frontier, each tiring hour gloomy with belief that the dream of a wonderful school that would give hope and a full life to the blinded children of France had been ended; and not knowing how exile would itself spread the innovations of Valentin Haüy abroad, so that, in time, recognition of the founder and honour to France would flow back from other lands.

The first indication of this was to come in Berlin. Word of Haüy's work had reached a Dr. Zeune, who had the ear of King Frederick of Prussia. Valentin Haüy was called to royal audience, persuaded to stay in Berlin to join with Dr. Zeune in establishing the first German school for blinded children on the lines of the one he had created in Paris. Heartened by this opportunity, Valentin Haüy spent the remaining months of the year in continuing service to sightless children. Then danger again threatened from

Napoleon's agents. Prussian forces were humiliatingly crushed at Jena, in November, and columns with the imperial eagles flaunted in the van were approaching. Valentin Haüy and the young Remi Fournier took to the road once more, again travelling eastward, again towards a fortuitous meeting that would affect the future of the cause of the blind.

Winter was on the Russian countryside when their carriage rolled into the town of Mittau, near Riga. By chance, also stopping overnight, was a prince of the blood, the exiled Comte de Provence, who, with the downfall of Napoleon, would be called back to his people as Louis XVIII. He talked with Valentin Haüy, garnering news of events in Paris, and learning of the fate of the institution that his ill-fated relative Louis XVI had supported in the pre-revolution years. From this meeting word went on to Czar Alexander, in St. Petersburg, who at once decided to emulate the French and the Germans, and to call on Valentin Haüy to spend his next years in establishing Russia's first school for blind juveniles.

The new era for the blind, thus opened,

soon reached into Belgium, Britain, Ireland, Austria and then America. Yet the true global harvest of the self-imposed mission rested on the survival of a sickly boy child in the cottage home of a village saddler, a child born in mid-winter three years after Valentin Haüy fled into exile along a nearby roadway.

2

The Blinded Child

LOUIS BRAILLE was born in the Commune of Coupvray, a village nestling against a hillside twenty-five miles east of Paris. In a lush corner of the Brie country embraced by an arm of the River Marne, the stone and daub cottage in which he was born—two rooms upstairs and two down—still stands in the lower, and flatter, part of the village and, though now refurbished as a simple museum, is little different from what Louis Braille knew as a child.

There are the same solid oak doors, massive stone chimney, wall oven in the living-room-kitchen, the same wooden stairs he climbed to bed at night, and outside the cottage is the iron arm that bore his father's trade sign as village saddler, *bourrelier*; all are still in place in surroundings of similar cottages in a little byway with the grand title of Chemin des Buttes.

Indeed, in the straggling village itself there is little sign of change. Coupvray escaped the outward thrust of the great capital. Untouched by surburban railways or multi-lane highways, it stands like a page from the past, with houses of slated roofs and dormer windows crouched along cobbled streets, and lanes showing no mark of the violent tides of wars or foreign occupation.

The visitor finds an ancient village, drowsy in daytime reverie, and the only noticeable post-war difference is in the hilltop square, named now after its most famous son, with his bust raised above bas-relief panels illustrating scenes from his life, looking across to the venerable grey-green church and throwing its shadow across an empty grave surmounted with a rough stone urn containing the bones of hands that "opened the doors of knowledge to those who cannot see".

The traveller finds those words, in French and English, on tablets attached to the walls of Braille's birthplace. This is at the foot of a steeply sloping cobbled lane locals call La Touarte, up which the village harness-maker, Simon-René Braille, carried his pallid one-day-old son on a wintry day in January 1809, to the village square to seek urgent registration at the Commune offices and later to a hurried baptism at the church. He was anxious for these dispensations before death might intervene and exclude the sickly child from both membership of the community and the faith that gave right of entry to heaven. The father was then a worried man, and there were firm grounds for his concern.

Simon-René Braille, born in 1765, had lived his life in the stone cottage in the Chemin des Buttes. He had learned the skills of harness-making from his father, Père Simon, who had worked for fifty years from the same oaken bench, still standing in the Braille cottage, in one of the two ground-floor rooms. At age twenty-seven Simon-René had married Monique Baron, of a local farming family, and it is of historical significance that— uncommon among villagers at that time— both husband and wife could read and write. From all accounts, Monique was comely, with brown eyes and a loving nature; Simon-René was a rounded man, round of face with a bulbous nose and back bent from years crouched over his moulds, shaping saddles and collars, and from countless hours of fine stitching of reins and harness. They were married in the village church on 5 November 1792, and a year to the day after, the first child, Catherine-Josephine, was born. (Each of their children would carry the name of a king or queen of the realm.) In the following years Monique gave birth to a son, Louis-Simon, born on 9 March 1795, and to Marie-Celine, born on 15 January 1797.

The first year of the Brailles' married life had been marred by public displays of bloodthirsty vengeance in Paris, including the beheading of King Louis XVI and his Queen, Marie Antoinette. The first three Braille children grew up in an age of revolutionary horror, of mobs rampaging city streets a mere thirty kilometres from their home, of daily executions, massacre of priests, raping of nuns, sacking and burning of convents and churches, all events of execration to the mind of their father. The village saddler had come to adulthood in a different social and national climate, and in early manhood he had seen life change suddenly and savagely.

Villagers across France, no matter how far from Paris, felt hammer blows of change. Deliberate Terror, imposed by the so-called Committee of Public Safety, spread across the land. *La grande peur* filled every commune, a great fear that emptied the countryside of nobility, wealthy land-owners, gentry and the élite; and the work and trade they had generated all but dried up. In Coupvray the impact on the lives of artisans such as Simon-René Braille was almost crippling. The château of the Princes of Rohan, poised on the hill-side behind the small vineyard Père Simon had planted, was vacated and lifeless. The big coaches and cabriolet no longer rolled through the village on their way to the château for week-long house-parties, thus halting the flow of harness replacements or repairs at the sign of the village *bourrelier*. The Marquis d'Orvilliers and his Marquise, Jeanne-Robertine, had followed the princes of the blood and fled to safer lands. Without that flow of work there was little more than servicing the harness of local peasant carts, the two-wheeled iron-shod tumbrils, already infamous for their use in Paris.

Rural life was hit even harder in the following years with the coming of the Consulate and Napoleon's rise to power. As the dictator's military adventures spread across Europe, so his Préfect agents scoured the countryside for men and stock to fill gaps in the ranks of his legions and to feed his marching armies. In the Marne region, the Préfect, M. de Jessaint, arrogant and heartless in his uniform of blue and silver and his tricorne hat draped with the revolutionary scarf, led forays into villages such as Coupvray. The mere sudden clatter of hooves on cobbles would arouse alarm, for this could presage not only confiscation of horses, sheep and cattle, but also of sons, fathers, brothers, liable to die on the many battlefields, leaving women and children without breadwinners in a time of widespread poverty and near famine.

Contemporary writing held in French national archives, letters written by notable people, tell of the impoverishment inflicted on country people by these circumstances. Vivid insight to the near-subsistence lives led by families of even a skilled and respected artisan such as Simon-René Braille can be gained from a visit to the cottage in Coupvray. The building is now lovingly restored—with the aid of overseas funds, mainly from America—but the walls are crumbling with age. There is the old granite slab, gouged to make a sink, set in the wall with a hole leading outside, the stone chimney with the little hearth at floor level, the brick oven built by Louis Braille's grand-father, the solid latched doors and the wooden staircase leading to the space under the roof where the children slept, and where the bags of wheat and barley flour were kept for making their whole-some bread, doubtless with attendant mice. Outside still hangs the wheel and tackle that were used to hoist the flour bags to the roof, near the arm that once bore the sign "Braille—Bourrelier".

In the living-room-kitchen—with the bedded recess in which father and mother slept, and in which the Braille children were all born—there is the long wooden chest that was a feature, an essential to all such rural families. After Monique's kneading and baking—usually carried out only every two or three weeks because of shortage of wood fuel—the precious loaves were stored, some to be eaten at each meal.

Bread then held a deeply rooted symbolism in the psyche of the common people of France and was truly the staff of life. In Paris the mob of angry, hungry women had besieged the Palace of Versailles, demanding, shouting, not for meat, or fruit, or vegetables, but for "Du Pain! Du Pain!"

Sadly, neither King Louis, nor Queen Marie Antoinette, nor the miscreants who wielded power in Paris could change adverse weather and make bountiful harvests; and few women in the crowded city had country cousins to provide flour, and no woodlands in which to gather fuel in the bitter winters when the river froze over.

Life was not so hard in the Braille home, though there, too, bread held the same important role in the diet. As well, winter and summer, a small fire was lit in the tiny hearth, and the smoke-blackened soup pot was hung from the metal hook for the few vegetables to simmer in stock to make daily soup. Sometimes there would be pieces of bacon to cook with beans—obtained from Simon-René's friend, the village grocer, René Coquelet —or some mutton, or even a *viande de porc* obtained from family connections. But, generally, the diet was severely simple. Simon-René, waking at first light when the sabots of the poor field workers clacked along the cobbles, would eat a piece of bread and drink a cup of wine —sometimes also eat a raw onion—before starting his day's work. At midday, and in the evening, there would be a bowl of soup and more bread.

A picture has also been drawn of the family gathered round the fireplace in the evenings, when the wooden *volets* were drawn across the narrow windows, the father reading from the Bible and all saying prayers before sleep. There would be nights when Simon-René would read the dire news from journals that René Coquelet obtained from the Commune office, such as the *Constitutionel* news-paper; and it is known how he would be deeply saddened. Simon-René Braille was a monarchist, born and bred in a royal France. Documents in the national annals, written in safety after Simon-René was dead and the monarchy briefly restored, show the village saddler could never have been that person demanded by the revolutionaries, "a true Citizen of the Republic". He remained a royalist despite the appeals of freedom, equality and fraternity. An educated observer wrote of him, with respect for his responsible and caring nature, that "he was a man obviously of the old order, belonging to the *ancien régime* of the Bourbons".

So it was that, as the saddler watched his three children grow into their teens, with all his inner doubt and concern for their future, that the family situation was changed, and drama and challenge were brought once again into their lives. It was early summer of 1808, when he and his wife, Monique, had long thought their family complete, that she informed him she was once again *enceinte*—she was to have another child. Another black cloud of worry hung over them. After a gap of almost twelve years Monique Braille had to face again the perils of pregnancy, at the age of forty-two years.

Mortality in childbirth, normally high from lack of understanding of infection at that time, was known to be even more frequent in women beyond their mid-thirties, and this would certainly have been known to the village *sage-femme*, old Madame Parivel, who served the villagers as midwife, and whose attendance at the birth was arranged by Simon-René. There could have been no ease of mind that summer of 1808, when in the dark of night or early hours Simon-René lay in the bedded recess with his pregnant wife. Yet worry was to be prelude to optimism and thankfulness. By autumn, when the grapes were fat and glistening from the first cold nights and Monique was heavy with child, the faith of the saddler brought trust. He is recorded as telling his teen-age children: "This child will be a blessing, a prop to our old age."

The child had been expected before the year's end, but Christmas had come and gone and the first snows of the new year were blowing on the cold winds before

Monique Braille felt the first stirrings of childbirth in her womb. From her experience, she judged it would be a difficult birth, and so, according to record, arranged for the two girls and Louis-Simon to stay during her confinement with the family of Simon-René's friend, the wine-maker, Matthieu Simmonet. The scene has been described of the last days of pregnancy in the cottage, with the worried father using scarce fuel prodigally to keep out the cold at this difficult time for his wife, and feeding her with hot soup and bread to build her strength against the ordeal to come.

Monique's intuition was correct. The birth did not come quickly or easily. From all accounts the baby had little energy and made only weak efforts to break into the world. The hours of strain and pain began on the third day of the new year and Simon-René called Madame Parivel to lend her skill and comfort.

The child was finally delivered at the fourth hour of the fourth day, in 1809. It was a boy-child, and he came into life quietly, without the fuss they had known with their first three children, no lusty kicking, no yelling from newly filled lungs. It was said he did not seem even to want to breathe, and that when the midwife slapped his thin buttocks the response was little more than a whimper.

There was anxiety in the cottage from the moment the infant was born. Small, scrawny, listless, showing no inclination to suck nourishment from his mother, he roused memories of cases in the two families of babies born to women late in child-bearing years, and others born in midwinter, who had not lived to see the first days of spring. Through the long day and night that followed the birth, the child lay quiet, still and silent in the arms of the mother; and when daylight came again Simon-René had reached a desperate decision, to carry the day-old babe out into the wintry air. It was a risk, but it was taken in a sense of duty and the belief the child should be a member of the Commune and of the Catholic Church, for the probable death might come quickly and make impossible such events.

The baby was wrapped in a blanket and carried against the saddler's chest up the sloping cobbles of La Touarte, first to the grocer's shop, to enlist his friend the village *épicier* as a witness, and then to the home of the wine-maker, Matthieu Simmonet, to show the baby's wan face to his sisters and brother.

Then, with Simmonet and René Coquelet as witnesses, he carried the child to the office of the Mayor of the Commune of Coupvray, only to find that official was absent in Paris, and to meet a disinclination in the deputy to register the baby there and then. However, Simon-René Braille's sense of urgency prevailed, and the Deputy Mayor, M. Moulin, agreed to make the entry in the Commune Register.

He noted the fact that he was making the entry in the absence of the Mayor and wrote:

. . . on the fifth day of January in the year of Our Lord, eighteen hundred and nine, at ten o'clock in the morning, appeared before us Simon-René Braille, aged forty-four, saddler, resident in Coupvray, who showed us a male child born yesterday at four o'clock in the morning of himself and his wife,

Monique (*née* Baron), to whom he wished to give the name Louis . . .

The formality was completed with signatures of the father and of the two witnesses, Coquelet and Simmonet. For the first time, the name of Louis Braille appeared in historical record. He was then only thirty hours old.

The child's first excursion, the act of registration, seemed to give little ease to the parents, and the baby's lassitude preyed on their feelings until the following day, when Simon-René again walked the slope to the church on the hill, there to press the curé, Abbé Pillon, to arrange an early christening in the firm reasoning that if the child should die before christening the soul might be barred from entering heaven. The Abbé listened to the request with understanding, and the ceremony was arranged for the fourth morning of the child's life, it needing a day to notify relatives in nearby villages, in Jablines and Chalifert, and places between.

Thus it was that on the morning of 8 January 1809, the four-day-old baby boy was carried once more up La Touarte to the village square and into the old church, where, clinging by a thin shred to life, he was given the blessing of holy water from the font of hewn stone (still standing to this day) and was admitted to the Holy Roman Catholic Church with the single name of Louis. His godfather, a farming relative from the village of Chalifert, also named Louis, wrote only his surname on the certificate of baptism, Michel. His godmother, Genevieve Boulingre, of a peasant-farming branch of the family, of Jablines, then put her full name to the church document. There was yet a third witness: above the signature of the curé, Abbé Pillon, the name of M. Petit. This was the elderly schoolmaster, who served the church as bellringer, tolling the *angelus* each afternoon, and who tended to clocks and the supply of blessed elements for services, in between working to instil rudiments of writing and reading into the few village children. In signing this certificate of baptism he laid claim to early interest in the life of a child who would be his most famous pupil.

The Braille family accepted without question the creed that the hand of God shaped all events in their lives—so strong was their faith. When, in the weeks following the baptism, the baby took nourishment from his mother's breast and began to grow stronger, they attributed this recovery to his admittance into the Catholic Church, and, with that trust, fear of losing the child began to fade. The weeks of winter, snow, slush—with northeast winds sending cold fingers round roughly fitting wooden doors—demanded precautions and careful nurturing, but each passing week saw the small baby making progress. From then on, the newborn brought joy to the home and was adored by sisters and brother alike, so that when spring brought soft rain and warmer days, Simon-René could look through the window from his workbench and watch the children play with the infant on the small square of grass.

One day, Louis-Simon took the horse for shoeing by the village farrier; he brought the old shoes home and, according to custom, nailed them above the back door of the cottage for luck. And luck and happiness seemed to fill that first summer of Louis Braille's existence. As he thrived, so sun and rain promised good harvests and heavy crops of grains, fruit and grapes, and Napoleon won a victory over the Austrians and, seeking a son of his own to carry on his imperial line, moved to dispose of his official attachment to Josephine and to marry another Austrian, Princess Marie-Louise, who would bear him his first son two years later. And the saddler, Simon-René Braille, had his son, growing bigger every day, the child he had said would be a prop to his old age. His children told friends how, one night at prayers, his eyes shining in candlelight, their father had spoken prophetically: "God sent this child to bring comfort to us all. Let us be thankful."

The long summer of 1809 forged a bond between Monique Braille and her baby son that would outlast all others. This tie, born in tenderness for the struggling infant in a woman giving birth late in her child-bearing years, would grow to final strength in the most trying period of Louis Braille's life. In that summer came the first signs of awareness in the child's eyes, indications of love and individuality, and the first faltering attempts at walking, the clutching of her fingers to save falling. Fear of losing this child in the beginning would have added to the mother's joy as the weeks wore away into autumn and grape clusters grew fat in the vineyard, bunches of wine-producing fruit that would have special significance in Louis Braille's mind in his last years.

With the coming of winter, as he continued to gain strength, and tight fair curls grew on the little head, Simon-René was able to spend more time with his baby son, and, together with Monique, marvelled at the sudden bright smile that lit the small face with unusual radiance. And not only Monique and Simon-René observed this gleam of brilliance in the boy's face. It was there for others to see, and some would attest to the bright smile in later writings. The warmth that shone forth many times in the child's first two years gave rise to belief in the family that there was something in the nature of this infant that reached out to others, a certain quality that would give strength, resolve and wisdom to mother and father in the trial that lay ahead.

During this time, Simon-René Braille began to keep the infant with him as he worked at his bench, at times seating him on the benchtop as he carved away at some wooden toy, a horse, a dog, a duck, and always there was sign of the acute sense of curiosity that would bring tragic consequences. In those months was fostered a fascination and admiration for the artisan father's strong hands and skill in shaping and cutting and sewing. It would never be known whether Simon-René saw any peril in this acute curiosity, or sensed the deep-laid wish to imitate the father. Untroubled, he would allow the boy to play in the workshop as he filled orders for harness and equippage. At night, with the family by the fire, the small boy would sit on his father's knee, oblivious to the meaning of news being read from Paris newspapers. He would have heard gossip, without any sense of excitement, of the massing of a great invasion force, of columns moving eastward towards the Polish frontier, imperial guards, cavalry, infantry, cannon and vast baggage trains; the Grande Armée on its way to conquer Russia. Nobody could foresee that early summer of 1812 how cold and distance would tear the heart out of Napoleon's mighty army, how history would be changed. And nobody could foretell how in the home of the village saddler of Coupvray a tragic accident would end in a triumph over dark ignorance that would cross more frontiers than Napoleon ever dreamed of reaching.

No written record has survived to detail the tragedy that struck the Braille family of the Brie village of Coupvray in mid-1812. Nothing in the Paris archives, in surviving documents and letters, nor in recollection of Louis Braille's conversations, gives anything more than a hint of the circumstances of the childhood accident, whose outcome was to touch the lives of millions of blinded human beings. Knowing, in hindsight, of the benefaction that was to grow from the childhood impairment, the failure of both mother and father, sisters and brother—all of whom could read and write—to record the event, was a grievous omission. The noted Parisian blind historian, Professor Pierre Henri (who taught for almost half a century in the very institute Valentin Haüy founded, who walked the same corridors and used the same rooms as Louis Braille) failed to trace even the precise date of the accident in the village saddler's workroom. Thus history is left dependent on reconstructions from local hearsay, from legend passed down among generations of relatives, neighbours and village families, and on what gossip emerged with which to describe this important accident.

Pilgrims seeking the facts of Louis Braille's blindness at his birthplace might hear conflicting accounts, such as that told at the cottage-museum to this writer, of how the three-year-old boy was left alone in his father's workshop on a Sunday while the family—father, mother, sisters and brother—walked the hill to mass at the old church. Against what is known of the character of Simon-René Braille and his sense of responsibility, this version not only appears unlikely, but to be more a product of imagination than fact. The village *bourrelier* was known to be a fine artisan, proud of his tools, which he normally kept hanging on a board behind his workbench—still there today—and out of reach of the child. It seems more than likely that the accident happened while the child was playing in the workroom and the father's attention was distracted, as one local legend suggests, by the news of Napoleon's Grand Armée crossing the Neimen to invade Russia.

Whatever the circumstances, it is clear that one day in the early summer of 1812 the little boy was left alone in the workroom, and with his acute sense of curiosity and armed by watching his father's strong skilled hands, he was urged to try and imitate the saddler's work. Somehow he was able to grasp a tool, probably left on the top of the bench, and again there is controversy. There is no certainty on the type of tool that came into the little hands. Some accounts hold that it was a bradawl, one of the holed type of instruments used to thread twine in sewing reins and harness. The version presented by the Braille museum, however, shows the child injured himself with a cutting tool called a *serpette*, a pointed knife shaped like a billhook used for slicing strips of leather for harnesses. In later years, out of a clouded memory, Louis Braille only spoke of the weapon that caused his blindness as a "sharp-pointed instrument".

Bradawl or *serpette* or any other kind of pointed tool, the wound was serious, and the shock to the child can be imagined. Cries of pain and terror would have brought the distraught parents rushing to meet dread reality, to find the three-year-old clutching his right eye with tears of pain and fright, and blood running between the fingers. And any hope that the lid or the eyebrow had been lacerated would have vanished when the hands were prised from the face and it was seen that vital juices, the very essences of sight, were oozing from the eyeball itself. The "sharp-pointed instrument" gouged deep enough in the eye to totally destroy cornea and pupil. The little orb through which had passed colour, vision of shapes and movement to the child's brain was utterly ruined. He would never see again through that one eye.

Consternation in the Braille family would have been made more acute by helplessness. With no hospital to rush to for aid, and turn as they might to some medico in a nearby township, they would be in the hands of nothing more than a bloodletter, an applier of leeches, a purveyor of palliatives and soothing words. Yet, not to disparage doctors of that era, it must be said that the finest battle surgeon in Napoleon's Grande Armée could not have restored sight to that butchered eyeball. Nor was there any hope of help from the local apothecary's lotions or herbs, and in this desperate strait the parents would have found a last resort in salves or ointments of imagined magic powers culled from rural legend. It was in those circumstances that the step towards final and complete blindness was taken.

There is a long history in rural France, as in many lands, of peasant people trusting in herbal wizardry, in travelling mendicants, and wise old folk claiming to know of magical healing substances selected from among a profusion of simple remedies for every ailment under the sun, of such things as applications of mutton tallow, calomel, beeswax, various common herbs, crushings of berries and a creamy concoction squeezed from the roots of the iris plant, which, legend said, was used by Roman legionnaires to heal their wounds.

Without doubt, whatever was applied to the injured eye laid the ground for extended tragedy.

In that medically ignorant era the most enlightened doctors knew nothing of a teeming micro-world of unseen infective organisms. This situation was undreamed of, and it would be more than sixty years on before another French genius, a namesake of the injured child—Louis Pasteur —would alert mankind to the existence of microscopic invaders of the human body, bacterial enemies to health and life. And without such knowledge how could there have been even rudimentary hygiene? Fingers, most certainly unwashed, would have prised open the child's eyelid and exposed the wound for close inspection; and, just as certainly, dabbing and bandaging would have followed with cloths not made sterile. Pasteur's discovery—a lifetime away in the future—could not have prevented the sad consequence. Defeat of sepsis awaited the twentieth century, with Domagk's sulfa drugs and the first true penicillin antibiotic, produced at Oxford by the Australian Howard Florey.

It was bitter irony that the tender ministrations of the distraught parents laid the basis for destruction of both eyes. Yet it had happened many times before. A thousand or so years earlier, the chronicler on primitive medicine, Agathias, had written: "The right eye when diseased oft gives its suffering to the left."

Agathias did not know why this was so, any more than the Braille family did. Whether total blindness in the case of the Braille child was due to infection or not must remain conjecture. Bacterial invasion of the wounded eye could have resulted in microbes eating tissues and procreating, thus moving through the cavernus sinus and reaching—and destroying—the ganglion of the optic nerve through which vision from both eyes has to pass to receptor cells, which present the complete picture to the brain.

Modern biological science—ophthalmology and immunology—however, now presents a staggering concept. This suggests that having ruined his right eye by his own hand, Louis Braille's own physiology—his body's defensive mechanism—went on to destroy his other eye!

This terrible fate is seen as a reversal of the natural defences against invading organisms, a turning of bodily protection against one's own tissues, which in the case of the eyes is known as "sympathetic ophthalmia". There is little that is sympathetic in this. The condition is the same as in the so-called auto-immune diseases, in which cells that police the body and destroy invading antigens—defenders, such as lymphocytes, macrophages and so on—attack natural cells, just as if they were invading bacteria and so destroy tissue and bodily functions.

All this knowledge was beyond imagination at the time of the child's accident; indeed, the process is not fully understood today. Thus it seems most likely that Louis Braille, the child, was victim of the condition that medical scientists describe as "self-attacking-self".

Whether Louis Braille was totally blinded by bacteria destroying the critical nerve ganglion, so blocking images from reaching the brain's receptor cells, or by the immune reaction attacking the retina in his good eye, it is most probable that his body produced billions of defender cells in an effort to eliminate the infection. This means he would at least have been unwell, and perhaps in fever, while still fighting against the shock of injury. Whatever the intensity of illness, it could have been a cushion against the awful fact of fading sight, and this helped to erase memory of the trauma from his mind.

What is certain is that total blindness would not have been sudden. Self-attacking-self is not a swiftly completed process, but the speed of the onset of blindness has been noted by the blind French savant, Professor Pierre Henri. He wrote:

We find ourselves faced with an obvious case of sympathetic ophthalmia, because, in spite of all the care that the parents have showered on the child, according to their account Louis Braille was *soon* plunged into complete darkness. And, as usually happens when blindness comes to one so young, he could not retain a mental picture of the world, not even his mother's face.

Louis Braille carried no memory of these

days of fading sight; yet, inevitably, there would have come the day in the summer of 1812 when, seeing her young son reach out a groping hand, the truth would have dawned on the distraught Monique Braille. Just as inevitably, for the three-year-old boy, the time would have come when he could no longer see his mother's face through the fog of impending blindness, when he glimpsed the last sight of blue sky, trees and the place of his birth. Finally, irreversibly, the bird of blindness would have spread black wings over all he had known in his three brief years of vision. Some time in that fateful summer Louis Braille lost the most precious of his senses.

Simon-René Braille carried remorse and contrition for the remainder of his sixty-seven years of life. He made that plain in all he said and did in relation to his blinded son in the times that followed the unguarded moment in his Coupvray work-room. Thus it seems all the more tragic that he was never to know the good that flowed from evil, the blessing that would flow from his son's impairment. It is apparent, indeed, that in the months after Louis became totally blind daily anguish would have been especially poignant for both father and mother. This would have been most intense at meal times, when food had to be spooned from the child's platter to his mouth, when his daily bread had to be broken into pieces that he could find with his fingers.

There would have been other reminders in the way the blinded boy adapted to his new dark world, and these, too, would have been a rebuke to the father. In the manner of the blinded young—now extensively catalogued by modern research—three-year-old Louis would take to holding his head forward and tilted to one side with his face drawn into serious concentration—as though trying to see with his ears. At times, in quiet contemplation, he would have sat in the small living-room-kitchen, as though far removed from the world, and then, as though puzzled, would have held his hands level with his shoulders, fingers sometimes flickering as though feeling the air, at other times exploring his own face, feeling his nose, his mouth, his ears and brow—seeking, as most blinded children do, some solidity for dark, formless existence.

When not engaged in these mannerisms and with his eyelids always closed, he would give little sign of being aware of his plight, and he would be so still and quiet, apart from small movements of hands and lips, that he would appear to be lingering in a dream world. And yet there would be times when he would respond to remarks that would strike a chord, and there would come a quickening in the manner and a glimpse of the delightful child the family knew before the disaster. Like a treasured memory the bright smile would suddenly light the now commonly serious face. Being rare, the radiance would have more appeal than before his blindness.

In the passing of months into years the condition of sightlessness would have seen young Louis become more oriented to being without perspective. His powers of concentration improved and brought new concern and demanded keen watchfulness by parents and sisters and brother as he began to find his way about the cottage. As with blind children generally, his agility would have been surprising—and it would have been hard for the family to understand that while no light, no colour, reached the boy's brain, yet he could store a form of blueprint for the location of chairs, table, fireplace—and the danger of burns—stairs and doors. The family might have been surprised—and it would have seemed wonderful—that he could find his way about with speed, with facility, without collision. Yet there was nothing unusual in orientation in a child blinded so early in life. There were hidden traps for the boy, such as the well that had been sunk against the wall just outside the back door to the cottage, but Simon-René and Monique kept a sharp eye when Louis went near the doorway. It was all natural adjustment, and it was just as natural that Simon-René became protective and worried over the future. How would his blind son live when his parents were no longer able to provide? What would he do?

There was no question but that Louis-Simon would follow his father in the trade of saddler, just as Simon-René had followed his father, but blinded Louis could never shape leather to form saddles and collars, or splice straight strips of hide to stitch into harness or long reins. No pride of craft, no artisanship for Louis; nothing more than simple fingerwork of plaiting strips of wool for coloured tassels to decorate completed sets of harness.

The future held little promise for Louis Braille.

As Louis Braille adjusted to his world of darkness a rapid tide of change swept across France, flooding through cities and villages alike. In the winter following the accident in the workroom of the saddler of Coupvray, the remnants of the shattered Grand Armée straggled back through the Russian snows to the Polish border. Of Marshal Ney's proud force of Imperial Guards, less than a thousand men survived. Napoleon left his broken forces to ride back to Paris to face dissent and a plot to sieze power on reports of his death. It was the plotters who died, executed, and the Emperor was again in control, with plans to raise a new massive army from the nation's towns and villages. Public dis-illusionment was too strong, however, even for Napoleon. A year later, the Legis-lative Body, a sycophantic assembly while

the Emperor was winning battles, produced unprecedented criticism:

> The *patrie* is under threat from all sides.
> We suffer destitution unmatched in
> our history. Commerce is destroyed!
> Industry is ruined! And what has caused
> these unutterable miseries? Vexatious
> administration! Despicable collection of
> taxes! Cruel recruitment for the armies!
> Barbarous endless war swallows the
> nation's youth—tears it from education,
> commerce, industry, and the arts . . .

The document proved a signpost to the
eclipse of the Emperor's powers. His
métier, invasion and conquest, was
displaced by the weight of national econ-
omics. He scurried south, disguised as an
Austrian officer, to escape assassination,
and to reach the Mediterranean island of
Elba. Church bells pealed across the land
to greet the man who returned as king, the
former Comte de Provence, the prince of
the blood who had been impressed with
the work of Valentin Haüy when both met
in exile in Russia less than a decade earlier.
Restoration of the Bourbon dynasty,

however, appeared to bring little relief to rural life. In the Marne region, the hated Préfect changed sides as readily as he had removed the red scarf of revolution from his tricorne hat and replaced it with the royal white cockade. The tax levies were still imposed on such trivia as salt, wine, playing cards and tobacco; still forcibly collected were cattle and stock. Further upheaval in the nation's affairs would be experienced before royal interest would touch the life of the Braille family. The blind boy was just six years old when this came about, when the bombshell of the Hundred Days fell upon France.

On 1 March 1815 Napoleon's disastrous revival began. Encouraged by widespread disillusion and discontent, he broke free of exile on Elba, landed on the south coast at Fréjus, and with a thousand veterans began his march on Paris, riding by way of Cannes and Grenoble, with opposition melting before him as he called on old soldiers to restore glory to *la belle France*. The following months are branded into history: spring and summer brought the final dénouement on the Belgian slopes of Mont-St-Jean, in the battle of Waterloo.

With his banishment to the remote and rocky Atlantic island of St. Helena came the occupation to enforce savage reparation, with Allied soldiers camped under trees in open spaces where the Champs-Elysées now run.

Small communities, such as the village of Coupvray, resounded to the boots of marching men. A violent era had ended, but a new and ugly period was pending. For the blind boy of Coupvray, sounds of hobnail boots on cobbles, strange voices speaking in a foreign tongue became a daily routine, which he would endure for the next three years.

The first years of childhood blindness would have been among the most difficult in Louis Braille's life. In a dark world, compelled to depend on sound and touch for human contact, he would have clung to his mother and father as a shield against the fearful depression that commonly strikes the newly blinded. There would have been times when he fell into the stance that modern specialists know as "posture collapse", which comes with mental isolation, with knowing he was "different". Indeed, in the cottage in which he was raised, there is now a museum setting that shows his effigy seated on a simple chair by the hearthside, a picture of utter sadness.

Louis Braille's plight, after all these years, is plain enough. Once the critical function of vision ended, the boy was faced with terrifying obstacles. His infant mind would no longer gain intuitive intelligence from other people's facial expressions. The black wings had blocked out his father's round face, his mother's brown eyes, her brows raised in rebuke or warning, the teasing smiles on his sisters' faces. Vision could no longer shape reaction and response; now his experience of the world rested on touch, smell, hearing and taste. There were legacies from the past to aid him; he could identify the pungency of onions chopped for daily soup; he knew the fragrance of freshly baked bread, the leather of his father's apron, the acrid smell of a burning candle. He knew because in those first months of blindness there were gossamer memories of the world he had vacated.

Yet, these too, along with shape and

colour, soon faded from recall and became first a memory of a memory, then nothing. They dissolved into blackness, as did the memory of sunlight on the Marne, and autumn gold on wheatfields that fed much of Paris. Then, as he grew older, there would be an end to the last scintillas of colour in his dreaming. His brain, busy in slumber, could relive only the now familiar sounds, smells and touch. Never again— sleeping or waking—would he know shape, colour or perspective.

To compensate, there began an acute development of his remaining senses. His ears, nose and, most of all, his fingertips, garnered the information of life about him in his capsuled world. He could read tenderness and sorrow in his mother's voice, he could detect awkwardness in the tones of visiting relatives and friends who avoided referring to his blindness, to his being different. In his new condition he heard words used that meant things he could no longer picture in his darkness: colours—red, green, blue, yellow; shapes and scenery—sky, trees, stars, hills. These were only words and held no visual meaning.

A further obstacle to adjustment was a sense of time. There could not be distinction between light and darkness. Day was night with sound: night was a time like day, with different noises—heavy breathing, someone snoring, wind against the cottage busy round the chimney, beams creaking. He was able to fit day sounds to activity; his father hammering, mother cooking, footsteps along the street belonging to people whose voices he knew, wheels on the cobbles, but, most of all, the different way people spoke between themselves and the way they spoke to him. The feeling would grow into conviction that, despite the love, kindness and pity he read into cadences and intonations of speech from people with seeing eyes, they never could—never would—understand the state of being blind.

Within a year of losing vision, Louis Braille the boy had oriented himself to his condition; but there were distractions and events that confronted him and which he would not fully comprehend. His elder sister, Catherine-Josephine, married and left home. There was solemnity at the church, sombre pledges, and then joyous celebration! There were evenings of serious talk between his mother and father, sometimes about his future, sometimes about events in Paris and the national danger; and there were other times, when his father taught him how to knot the strips of coloured wool into fringes for harness he was making. Then a great change came over the life of the family. In the aftermath of Napoleon's vainglorious Hundred Days had come the Allied Army of Occupation. France had to meet reparations of some 700 million francs—an enormous sum for the time—and foreign troops were in place to see the nation paid its debt for the disruption Napoleon's empire had caused. The village of Coupvray was chosen as a base for part of the Imperial Russian Army; troops were foisted upon most local homes.

Three or four peasant soldiers were billeted at the Braille cottage. They slept on straw in the cellar, drank the saddler's wine, ate meals with the family, but provided no bread or other victuals. The six-year-old blind boy was confronted with tests for his ability to adjust, challenges for his imagination. He would hear heavy boots clumping in and out of the cottage, a torrent of words in a strange guttural language, which sounded harsh against his mother's soft and liquid French, and the rough laughter of victors in the home of the conquered, separated always at the meal table from his family by unintelligible exchanges, by lack of understanding. The impact of this experience, lasting three years, on the budding intelligence of a gifted child is incalculable. The Russians were battle-hardened veterans who had marched a thousand miles in snow and rain to crush Napoleonic France. And since blindness had long banished memory of faces and features and expression, the boy could not picture unkempt hairy men in drab uniforms as they sat laughing and talking at the saddler's table and chewed bread and drank the wine of the vanquished. The men were sounds, without shape; these were voices giving stress, rise and fall, to words with no meaning and, perhaps, revealing nuances to the blind boy's acute hearing of being alien to the village, even expressing longing to be in some other simple home far to the east of France. Whatever the impact on the growing boy's mind of Russian soldiers spending three years in his home, not all their voices together would register on the young mind and shape the life to come as the new voice he heard in the home during the first year of the Occupation.

This voice was rich with expressive power, brimming with confidence, warm of tone, but at the same time strong with the ring of authority. This was the voice of the church. It belonged to a priest who had replaced Abbé Pillon, the curé who had baptised Louis Braille when only four days old. The new curé was a former Benedictine monk, from the famed Abbey of Cluny, and his appearance matched his voice. Abbé Jacques Palluy was a squarely built man, full-faced, with deep-set dark eyes that glowed with intelligence and sympathy. His greying hair curled back over the monk's hood he continued to wear.

He was devout and dedicated in his mission of saving souls from the clutch of the devil.

It is not clear whether Simon-René called on the new curé for help and advice, or whether the priest found heaven had blessed his new commitment with a golden opportunity, a sweet-faced, gentle boy, cloaked in earthly darkness, who could be locked for life into the radiance of God's love. From what is recorded, it is plain that Abbé Palluy brought Louis Braille into the embrace of the faith, a virgin soul to be instructed in the tenets of the Holy Roman Catholic Church, to be shown The Way, The Truth, The Light. He guided, encouraged and taught; and remarkably— if coincidentally—at the same time the father began his first instruction in the structure of language.

The primary education of Louis Braille began with upholstery studs knocked into strips of wood, forming letters of the alphabet. These first simple tools of instruction are now simulated in the Braille cottage-museum, and the authority for this crucial method of original teaching is cited by the curator and author, Jean Roblin, as coming from a contemporary of Simon-René Braille, a fellow saddler in a nearby community. What is significant in this simplified method of teaching the boy's mind the shape of letters of the alphabet, through touch, is the similarity to the approach used by Valentin Haüy in his pioneer work with the beggar boy, François Lesueur, which led to the world's first school for blind children.

However, while M. Haüy used single wooden blocks for each letter, Louis Braille's fingers were set to explore ten letters at a time on each wooden strip, three in all with five letters on the last one plus numerals. (The letter W, rarely used in the French language, was omitted as it would be at first in the code, yet to be invented.) Just as Valentin Haüy had done with his first pupil, so Simon-René did with his blind son. Fingers were guided to trace the shapes of letters; and as each shape was traced by feel, so the name of the letter was spoken, hour after hour, together at first, and then by the boy alone, again and again, over and over, so that despite the distraction of foreign voices, of soldiers of occupation in the cottage, the groundwork of learning was laid.

Concern for his son's future, doubtless fed by remorse, drove Simon-René Braille to persist with the simple alphabet-board tuition. At cost to his own work, he persisted in teaching Louis the alphabet, and then, just as Valentin Haüy had done some four decades earlier, he faced the problem of converting knowledge of the alphabet into simple words. Now his patience was further extended, in daylight and in the evenings, in guiding the boy's hand in writing letters with pen and pencil, joining them together into short simple words, in wavering script. When the alphabet boards were finally put aside and the simple writing was completed, Simon-René Braille had made his gift to future generations of sightless beings. Not just that he had laid the groundwork for his son to read and write—after a fashion. No! It went farther and deeper than that in the outcome. He had begun to develop a sensitivity in the boy's fingertips that grew more and more acute with practice and to train a retentive memory, which, with the sense of touch, would carry the name of Braille across the globe.

There was a limit to what the father could teach the blind boy. Aptitude and unusual ability soon made it plain to both

Simon-René and to the consulting Abbé Palluy that the young mind was ready to be weaned to a wider scope, and it was decided to press for a place at the one-room village school. Thus he came under the hand of the man who had signed his certificate of baptism, bellringer and teacher, the elderly M. Petit. So each weekday the boy would climb the La Touarte cobbles to the square that would one day bear his name. At first his brother, or a sister, would guide him, but very soon he was finding his own way back and forth. In class he showed the same quick adaptability. He began to compete with sighted scholars; in oral tests he was superior, his superb memory registering every word, every fact, and though he was slow in writing, having to guide his pencil between lines of string to form words, power of concentration and his application helped him to greater confidence. But he was always handicapped by being unable to read, as did the others.

Almost a century and a half later, in June 1952, Helen Keller walked the same cobbles Louis Braille had trodden in his boyhood days to and from school. Among pilgrims from many parts of the world who come to pay tribute at Louis Braille's birthplace, she observed:

. . . judging from the brilliance of mind he displayed at school, I can picture him as an exceptionally bright little boy, full of curiosity concerning everything he could touch. Besides, he was blessed with affectionate parents, and I feel sure he responded to their love as a plant does to sunshine.

Each fact, all the evidence, confirms the tenderness and devotion Simon-René and Monique Braille felt for their handicapped son, and yet that love came near to closing the door on all that he was to do in life.

Apart from normal school studies, young Louis Braille also received instruction from the former Benedictine monk, Father Jacques Palluy. It is certain that the Abbé worked hard to illuminate the darkened mind, to impart strength through faith, to develop forbearance, serenity and persistence; and, at base, to imbue a lifelong credo of frugality, modesty and morality.

While this was customary shaping of character, it soon became apparent that the priest knew he was dealing with a mind of unusual promise, and this led to steps that would transform the future for the saddler's son. And, simultaneously with this development of relationship between village curé and the blind boy, there were changes in national and local affairs that would bring further influences to bear.

The Napoleonic era had ended. King Louis XVIII was firmly on the throne again, and *la grande peur* was a darkening memory; fear was gone from the countryside and the cities, life could again be pleasant and safe, even though the Allied Army of Occupation was still in place. The rich, the gentry, the landowners began to return from exile, *émigrés* who reclaimed positions of authority came back to occupy their castles and mansions. In Coupvray the château of Rohan was reopened, the Marquis and Marquise d'Orvilliers resumed their suzerainty over the surrounding estate and took up again their interest in local affairs. One other change in the village also helped shape Louis Braille's future. The aged schoolmaster,

M. Petit, was replaced by a younger and eager-minded teacher, M. Antoine Becheret. Thus there were influential people again in Coupvray, and the Marquis and Marquise, the Abbé and the bright young schoolmaster were bound to meet and to talk. Documentation in the present cottage-museum indicates that the conversation between them included Louis Braille's ability, and that this shaped Louis Braille's future, both in Coupvray, and in Paris.

At Versailles, King Louis remembered his meeting in exile with Valentin Haüy and had made known his interest in the school founded by the benefactor; the Minister for the Interior formed a departmental committee to which a court nobleman, Count Alexis de Noailles, was appointed chairman (and this gives rise to a suggested connection with the Marquis d'Orvilliers). The Count's committee acted swiftly in the royal interest: blind children, boys and girls, languishing in the squalor of the hospice for aged blind derelicts to which Napoleon had committed Haüy's school in 1800, were removed to an old dilapidated building on Rue St-Victor, half-way between the Latin Quarter and the Botanical Gardens, the same building that had been used as a prison during the revolution and in which Valentin Haüy's brother had been incarcerated.

By this time, along with other *émigrés* who had escaped oppression, Valentin Haüy had returned to his native Paris. However, he was not invited to resume directing the school for blind juveniles. Now it was a state institution, again decorated with the "Royal" appellation and supported by public money, so its operations were guided by departmental officials. As well, Valentin Haüy was then in his seventies, and known to be a favourite with the King. In government corridors in those days, royal favour was a shackle, for the King's interest was repugnant to public servants who had mainly won their places during the revolution era. Whatever the reasons offered, the management committee made no approach to the now lonely figure of the founder, but instead appointed, as director and administrator, a certain Sebastien Guillié, a doctor, who would show himself to be a self-satisfied pedagogue more inclined to impose strict discipline and control behaviour than to be concerned with the well-being and bodily health of the young blind.

The annals, public and institutional, reveal much of Dr. Guillié's administration of the establishment in the Rue St-Victor, but leave blank the reasons for unusual steps he took from time to time. Nothing explains how, late in 1818, he came to learn of the existence of the blind son of the saddler of Coupvray. There are indications in Coupvray that Marquise d'Orvilliers took a warm interest in the boy, and that her interest was made known through undisclosed channels to the doctor-director.

It is known that among the guidelines for admission to the establishment on Rue St-Victor, the management committee had stressed that every effort would be made to enrol at least one blind juvenile from each region of France, but this does not explain how Dr. Guillié came to know of the ten-year-old Louis Braille. All that is certain is that late in October 1818 he was moved to write to Simon-René Braille, saddler of the village of Coupvray.

The month of October 1818 brought joy and relief to the people of the Brie village. The day had come, with miraculous speed, it seemed, when the Allies decided France had met her debt. The savage reparations had been paid, and the punitive military occupation was to end. In villages such as Coupvray daily life could go back to its former privacy and quiet. One day the Russian soldiers paraded in the square and began their long march back to Russia. The church bell tolled, and the people happily waved *adieu* to the troops who had filled their homes. The heavy boots clumped on the cobbles for the last time, hidden wine was brought out in celebration, and life went back to normal with hopes of peace and prosperity under the fat Bourbon monarch. For Simon-René and Monique Braille, however, peace of mind lasted but a few days. Their serenity ended when the mail cabriolet from Meaux halted under the saddler's swinging sign, not for harness repairs, but to deliver an official-looking letter from Paris. The letter was headed. "Ministry of the Interior—from Doctor S. Guillié Director, Royal Institute for Blind

Juveniles". Formally, and impressively, it expressed greetings, and then stated: "So, I have to inform you that a place can be provided at this institution for your son, Louis, if certain conditions are met."

The parents' initial opposition and their doubts were made obvious by the flow of letters that followed. In the circumstances, their quandary can be understood. The girls were married and Louis-Simon was about to marry; they had this last child whom they had hoped would be a comfort and a prop to old age and found the prospect of losing him to an institution hard to accept. Although he was blind, the boy was loving, gentle, kind, and the cottage would be cruelly empty if he went away to what they could see was little more than an asylum. Here in Coupvray he had a home and was sure of his daily soup and bread. What could he get by going to this place in Paris? More words, more knowledge? How would that give him a living in the future?

Nothing is known of the pressure that was obviously brought to bear on the saddler and his wife, or by whom. All that is certain is that letters flowed back and forth between Dr. Guillié and the Braille cottage, letters questioning, letters answering, telling of conditions, letters expressing the parents' doubts. Weeks passed, the winter days grew shorter, until, late in December, opposition by the parents finally yielded to argument. Simon-René and Monique agreed, at last, that it was best for the boy's future for him to extend his education away from home. In the new year, Simon-René wrote the letter of acceptance, making the point that he would obtain a certificate of poverty from the Mayor of the Commune, and so would be absolved from paying school fees. The date on the letter was 4 January 1819. It was the boy's tenth birthday.

In Paris the acceptance was passed through channels and approved, and eleven days after the letter was written, on 15 January 1819, Director Guillié made the entry in the institute register of an expected new inmate. It was the first time the name of Louis Braille was written into the records of the establishment in which he would spend the rest of his life.

3

Shadow of a Saint

IN winter the stage coach would roll
out of Meaux soon after first light for
the jolting stop-start journey to Paris.
Given no undue delays—heavy snowfall,
icy roads—some four hours later it would
rattle with a clatter of hooves and iron-
shod wheels on the first of the city cobbles,
at the customs post set in the wall Parisians knew as the "Farmers' General".
There, after hours in the draughty wooden
carriage, passengers would alight to face
customs inspection before passing into the
city proper. Simon-René Braille rode with
his son on this coach on a wintry day in
February 1819. They left the cottage in the
still dark morning, and the boy started the
longest journey of his life. The swaying,
bucking stage coach, the sound of hooves
of the four-in-hand along the gravel road,
the crack of the whip, were all new
sounds, new experience. He was making

his first journey along the only road he would ever travel in life, and in death.

Chilled to the bone, joints stiff, Simon-René Braille left the customs post, his blind son clutching his hand, to find his way south of the river to the building in the Rue St-Victor. Together they trod through a Paris now long vanished, through narrow streets with the huddled houses propped against each other showing the neglect of four decades of revolution, with dark, canyon-like alleyways, all filled with sound: street criers, hawkers, barrowmen, coach wheels and hooves, and the strident voices of people compelled to live too close together. Native talent had yet to give birth to the great explosion of creativity—in art, music, literature, imaginative design and architecture—from which would evolve the great metropolis.

They crossed the river to the termination of the wide Faubourg St-Germain and, mid-way between the Botanical Gardens and the Latin Quarter, they came into the old Rue St-Victor, a grey, gloomy street smelling of mud on the river bank. And here waited the shock for Simon-René Braille's seeing eyes: the building in which his son would be incarcerated. Assurances dinned into his ears, perhaps by Abbé Palluy, by the eager Antoine Becheret, words from the serious Marquis, and written by the Director, could fade into disquiet, and doubts rise anew. Everything here was alien to the soft rolling country of the Brie, to the neat cottages of Coupvray.

The "new home" of the Valentin Haüy foundation was an age-old pile rising five floors from the street, its grim face bristling with cowled windows criss-crossed with iron bars and closed like sightless eyes. A frowning edifice, crouched around great double doors of metal-studded oak under a massive stone lintel, it had the glowering, forsaken look of what it had been during the ugly years of revolution, a prison. In this place, Simon-René had been assured, Louis would obtain an education and skills that would give him a better chance in life; in this drear building his young son would spend years. But he had made the decision and could not go back on his word just because the facade of a building was unattractive.

The sound of the heavy iron knocker echoing in dark space behind the massive doors brought an aged concierge, M. Demezière, who, learning their names, led them into the dank atmosphere of the interior, and up a creaking wooden stairway to a gloomy landing with bare boards to attend an audience with the Director. After a brief wait a command sounding through the thick door bid them enter, and they walked on a straw matting into a room where the Director sat behind his desk, a narrow, barred window behind him.

This was a scene of historic significance: the Director, brow furrowed, poring over the certificate of poverty from the Mayor of the Commune of Coupvray; the village *bourrelier*, an honest, plain man, but awkward and uncertain in the presence of authority, shifting from foot to foot, holding the blind boy's hand; Dr. Guillié dipping quill in ink and making the most important entry he would ever make in his blotted career in the school register: "Louis Braille, aged ten, of the village of Coupvray in the Seine-et-Marne Department, registered on 15 January, was admitted to the Institute this day of our Lord, 15 February 1819."

The boy was listed as number 70 in the register of pupils. There was the practice of a brief homily on aims and rules, on clothing that would be issued, on behaviour and effort, about staff and religious instruction, and that music studies were compulsory. In that small ceremony in the first-floor room of the old building, its history as yet hidden from the new pupil, Louis Braille, to be, arguably, the most famous blind man in history, was made a charge of the Institut Royale des Jeunes Aveugles. His father's role was ended. There was no more for Simon-René to do but comfort his son in parting and give parental advice, maybe: "Au revoir, my Louis. Be obedient. Try hard and do your best. I shall come in August to bring you home for the summer."

The misgivings Simon-René carried home to his wife that winter day of 1819 would have been sharpened to alarm had he known the severity of the routine his beloved son had entered. Hidden from the Braille family were the subsistence diet, the cold and discomfort in an ancient structure contaminated with a malady that would extract a mortal price for the immortality his son would give the family name.

Student number 70, aged ten, youngest among some seventy-odd blind children in the Institut Royale des Jeunes Aveugles was under the control of a disciplinarian who came close to being a martinet. His régime was firm to the point of being oppressive; it was frugal, strict and limited freedom of movement; it inflicted punishment with the rod and solitary confinement—blind children being locked in unlit cupboards and fed only bread and water for days on end—for minor breaches of rigid rules. Dr. Guillié wore several hats —Doctor, Director, Teacher, Guardian, Chief-of-Staff—and wore them conscientiously on behalf of the governing committee and the Ministry of the Interior, to both of whom he would supply glowing reports of his management, his kindness and his success. But, hidden from those bodies—as the rigour of the régime was hidden from Simon-René Braille—was the lack of true humanity, the calculating mind typified in the Director's banishment of the aged M. Valentin Haüy, to whom he denied the right to visit the institute he had founded.

If the reason for this heartless decision was based on maintaining discipline, it would have been the same as Dr. Guillié's excuse for the heavy hand he kept on the pupils. His annual reports show how much he was obsessed with discipline; that this rose from the conditions that he claimed to have met when he took control of the former institute for blind juveniles.

When the children were plucked from the squalor of the Quinze-Vingt hospice for aged blind derelicts to which Napoleon had committed them in 1800, they were, the new Director reported, "half-wild, dirty and dishonest, and with no respect for authority". The purpose of the institute had been eroded by the wanton neglect. Dr. Guillié wrote in his official report:

As on fallow land, no fruit was garnered during those mournful years. The blind children produced nothing but sterile expense for the government; and it was, with some personal pain, that I found the most effective way of reforming the situation was to expel many of the undisciplined pupils.

The future of the blind children the Doctor sent packing was never recorded; those who were left were from that time on dragooned into a life of continuous study, utter obedience and unquestioning respect, all their movements monitored, all their actions watched. Discipline and good order were more important than the foul state of the building in which they all lived, of higher priority than health. The Director was convinced that blind young persons needed a special type of control, and he was not averse to his attitude being widely known; for in his report to the Minister of the Interior in the year Louis Braille was inducted into his routine, Dr. Guillié wrote:

It has been clearly shown that the blind are not like other people. They are not liable to be restrained by external demonstration, which they cannot see, and thus can only judge things by extremes. They can know justice only by its effects, and so a paternal justice has been imposed to replace the previously weak system, which for too long has prevented good being done.

The dictatorial approach to the problem of the sightless affected inmates of the institution from the time the Doctor took control. Blind boys and girls, all in the same dark world, all part of the same organisation, all hoping for improvement and living in the same building, were utterly segregated, shut away from each other behind thick stone walls, and denied any contact on pain of expulsion, the loss of a future. As early as 1816, in his first year, Guillié had stated his opposition to association between blind boys and girls: "The sexes are completely separated. Any communication between them is not favoured and blind couples will not be admitted to this institution under any circumstances. They would be a constant source of discord and misunderstanding."

Yet boys and girls alike were subject to the same rigorous schedule, severe discipline and strict supervision. Their correspondence, incoming and outgoing, had to pass through the hands of the Director. All pupils slept in cold, dank dormitories on straw mattresses laid on wooden bunks, from which they were roused at six each day, no matter the time of year. A piece of bread, a drink of water, assembled prayers, and the schedule of classes would start at seven every morning and last through until eight in the evening, allowing only a break for a midday meal. And the judicious Dr. Guillié claimed to have mixed the lessons kindly, so that periods of difficult study would be followed by the "easy relaxation of manual instructions".

By early 1819, when Louis Braille came to the institute, the Director could claim to have control over behaviour, efficiency and economy, even down to the size and content of meals the juveniles were given to sustain life and energy. He had a set menu posted on the wall, which stated the food that would be served each week, and said this allowed pupils to complain if the kitchen staff did not meet the orders. This diet gave every blind child half a litre of soup and a few ounces of some kind of meat, once a day, with a small glass of wine twice a week. On alternate Sundays the soup was replaced by a roast, mutton or veal, with which, it was claimed, there were "generous servings of potatoes, onions or carrots". The Doctor went to the trouble of—and took pride in—relating how the daily soup was prepared. Some 40 litres (about eight gallons) were produced from two hooves of veal, 12 kilograms (some 29 pounds) of meat, and a few ounces of gelatine; and to avoid monotony dried vegetables or fresh vegetables cooked in dripping were added. This was the staple diet at the institution. He reported: "We were careful in making the daily meal both pleasant and substantial and it is proved a success because our children are so chubby."

The deception in the report was typical and would be exposed as a sham on later inspection by experts. It disregarded malnutrition and imperilled health from deplorable living conditions. In fact, the Director not only ignored the decaying surroundings of the institute, he took pride in recounting selected details, of interest to him, from the long history of the building. Unwittingly, in this, he made a contribution to the character of the boy whose talent would bring the institute wide renown.

Nobody then knew, nor does anyone know now, how truly ancient was the building that housed the institute for blind juveniles in the early decades of the nineteenth century. There is reason to suspect that it was the original home of the Collège des Bons-Enfants, the charity orphanage that was founded about AD 1250 and which built a sad reputation for a high death rate among children. What is certain is the pile was already ancient when it emerged into clerical history, in 1624, when the towering personality of Vincent de Paul (to be among the most famous of saints) took charge of the college and lived and worked and created new Orders from his place in the rotting structure that would house the first known institute for blinded youngsters. From his room on the first-floor-front, Vincent de Paul (he would be canonised a century after his death in 1660 and become the patron saint of charity) wrote countless dozens of letters to far corners of the Christian world in forming his Congregation of the Missions, the Order that later became known as the Lazarists. The saint had walked these cold corridors, had trod the same creaking wooden stairs, prayed in the same chapel and held council in places that became classrooms for the blind. On that first floor, where Louis Braille stood with his father under Dr. Guillié's scrutiny, Vincent de Paul had heard from Louise de Marillac how the vision of her future mission had come at Pentecost during mass at the church of St-Nicolas-des-Champs. In this building they had planned the work of charity they believed God had ordained, creating the unique Order of the Sisters of Charity, dedicated to the world's poor and oppressed. The wide-winged coifs of that army of women would make them known in many lands as the "aeroplane nuns".

The inmates of the blind institute were told that they trod where the saint had walked; and they were constantly re-minded how they lived in the shadow of the patron saint of charity, who had also been adopted as the patron saint of their institute. In their devotions in chapel, dedicated to St. Firmin, at every service the name of Vincent de Paul was mentioned, by visiting Lazarite priests and by churchmen from the nearby St-Nicolas-du-Chardonnet, a sprawling edifice on Faubourg St-Germain, where Louis Braille would be confirmed. The blind children were taught how St. Vincent had left this building in 1634 to go to St-Lazare, which gave its name to his Order, but that this did not end the association, since around a half a century later the old college was turned over to the Lazarists for training young priests vowed to a life of poverty and frugality. The building then had become known as St-Firmin Seminary, from the doors of which thousands of young committed men went out to serve in many corners of the world.

Dr. Guillié relished these connections with the hallowed names and the work of service to humanity, but never detailed to his pupils how the life of the seminary was brought to a brutal and bloody ending. He referred only to the "vile desecration of a holy centre of silence and prayer". And once, publicly, he lamented: "Oh, why did this building, full of memories of a good and holy man with all its joys of supernatural happenings, become the theatre for deplorable excesses and debauchery?"

The tale of excesses and debauchery connected with this building, as with the name and role of Valentin Haüy, were left hanging like shadows in the mind, and only the goodness and the exemplary life of Vincent de Paul was expounded by the Director. He told the boys of the life of the saint, how he was born into a large family, son of a poor shepherd, had been captured by corsairs when he was young and made a slave in the galleys of North Africa, how he had escaped to Italy, became a priest to serve the family of the powerful Cardinal Gondi, had been appointed chaplain to the house of Queen Marguerite of Valois (the repudiated wife of Henry IV) and how, as chaplain to the royal galleys, his compassion for the slaves of the oars had been legendary. Dr. Guillié would relate how Vincent de Paul, as head of the Collège des Bons-Enfants, ever busy writing his letters to missionaries in foreign lands—in Ireland, Poland, Prussia, Italy, America, Scotland—still gave time and alms to people in trouble. The Director would take a boy by the hand at times and lead him along a wall at the side of the courtyard (which had been covered

**LA COMMUNE de COUPVRAY
GARDE PIEUSEMENT
DANS CETTE URNE
LES MAINS
DU GÉNIAL INVENTEUR**

A rough concrete box bolted to the empty grave in Coupvray contains the hands of Louis Braille. Coupvray 'piously' will guard the hands of the genius inventor'.

A century passed after the burial of Louis Braille in a simple village churchyard before he was recognised by the nation and his bones – minus the hands – were followed by the President and visitors from all over the world to the Panthéon, resting place for heroes of France.

DANS CETTE MAISON
EST NÉ
LE 4 JANVIER 1809
Louis BRAILLE
INVENTEUR DE L'ÉCRITURE
EN POINTS SAILLANTS
POUR LES AVEUGLES

IL A OUVERT
À TOUS CEUX QUI NE VOIENT PAS
LES PORTES DU SAVOIR

IN THIS HOUSE
ON JANUARY 4 1809
WAS BORN
Louis BRAILLE
THE INVENTOR OF THE SYSTEM OF
WRITING IN RAISED DOTS FOR USE
BY THE BLIND

HE OPENED THE DOORS OF
KNOWLEDGE TO ALL THOSE
WHO CANNOT SEE

A tablet on the wall of the cottage where the Braille family lived for generations tells of the significance of the place for millions of blinded people.

Beneath this simple gravestone in the cemetery at Coupvray lay for a century the remains of Louis Braille. His bones, minus the hands, were reinterred in the Panthéon, in Paris, in 1952.

Foucault's so-called Piston Board answered Braille's deep-felt need to communicate with sighted people. It has been acclaimed as forerunner to the Braille typewriter.

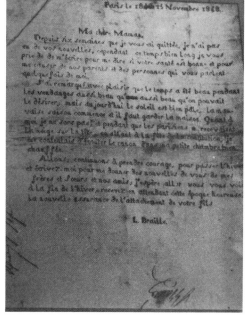

A letter written by Louis Braille to his mother on the Keyboard Printer, a joint invention with Pierre Foucault.

The Braille *planchette* with framed sliding grill. Three lines of windows provide for exact placing of the critical dots of the alphabet with a small stylus, which means the writing is done in reverse so that – below – the reading fingers can proceed from right to left.

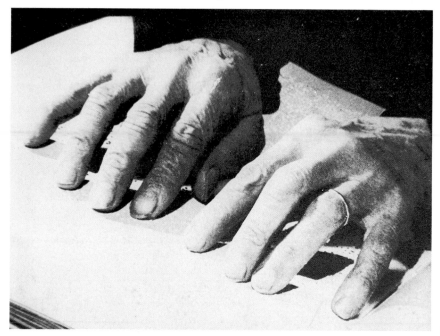

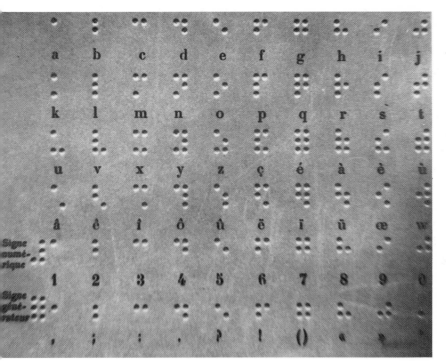

The Braille alphabet was based on the 'domino six' pattern, which fits the fingertips. It was devised by the sixteen-year-old inventor-genius, using a tool similar to the one with which he had blinded himself as a child.

A more modern version used by the British Royal National Institute for the Blind.

Jouffrey's original bust of the genius-inventor was made in 1852 from the death mask; the fingers of generations of blind French students have 'read' the features.

In London's Royal National Institute for the Blind,
Braille's bust has pride of place with the founder,
Dr. Armitage.

This daguerreotype made in the earliest days of photography is the only known likeness of Louis Braille taken during his life.

and converted into sectors for handcrafts, making cane chairs, knitted goods, shoes, baskets) and tell how this was once part of a daily walk the saint had followed.

"Not far from here, at the end of the Rue des Fosses St-Bernard," he would tell them, "was an old tower of confinement for men sentenced to deportation, or to work in the galleys; and our patron saint had a path cleared from here so he could make his way each day to bring gifts and consolation of the love of God to those poor men."

His voice was always solemn when speaking of the great man, and he would recount details of the room where Vincent de Paul had slept and worked, which was directly above the bathroom that the boys were allowed to use—once each month—and he would draw a vivid picture: "A wooden crucifix stood on a plain table; there was a straw mat, a cot and two chairs and nothing else. Those were the saint's sole possessions, and they were kept sacred, carefully preserved in the room that only Lazarite priests were allowed to enter before going on overseas missions—until some thirty years ago."

He did not tell his audience what happened to change the room, how the relics disappeared, except to wish: "After so many evils, may this building become again what it had been in the hands of our holy founder."

For the young blind boys the reverence in the voice of the all-powerful Director who guided all their futures transformed the memory of the long-dead saint into a warm and living presence; and in the dark of their minds the spirit of Vincent de Paul still walked the stairs and corridors with them each day of their lives.

From the time the metal identity disk, embossed with his number, 70, was pinned to his uniform, Louis Braille faced daunting difficulty in his new institutional life. He was not allowed to move without his disk and at first had to be guided by a sighted pupil, one of a half-dozen lads given places at the institute as guides and to help blind pupils with their writing of reports or letters, all of which went through the Director's hands. The help was short-lived, and the village boy had soon to find his own way along winding corridors, up and down stairs to different classrooms and workplaces, finding steps that led to mealtimes in the refectory, which was awkwardly sited in a gallery on the ground floor and could be approached from both sides. Quickly he had to fix in his memory a blueprint of the five floors with passages going off here and there, corridors cut into two to form narrow classrooms, and anterooms where Dr. Guillié had had eighteen looms set up for weaving cloth from which the boys' winter, summer and Sunday uniforms were made.

The blueprint in the mind would serve him, but a sixth sense also had to be developed in the frustratingly irregular edifice. In those first weeks, Louis Braille would slide a hand along the walls—old stones weeping with mildew—and be always careful because passages on different floors ran in differing directions. He needed to be constantly alert, ever straining to hear if he was walking into a blank wall, listening for the change of echo that would tell him when the stairs would fall away under his feet.

His hearing and his brain were forced to

come to terms with other sounds, the sounds of many voices. There was a special problem for the lad raised in the small Brie village. By ministerial edict, places at the institute had to be given to blind children on a basis of one for every region of the country. As near as was possible there was not to be two blind children from the same locality, and so many spoke their own *patois*. Local dialect, with special meanings and expressions, added to the problem of associating a voice with a name. As for all blind children, Louis Braille could have no flash or recall triggered by the shape of the head, by a smile, by colouring, or size. Only his keen ears could recognise a person and the memory identify, swiftly, accurately.

Louis Braille grew accustomed to the rambling spaces, to the sound of voices, to finding his way to his desk, to his locker and to his bunk in the dormitory, all of which held the embossed number 70. And he grew used to being cold and hungry. As with food, Dr. Guillié economised on wood fuel; the pot-bellied stoves on each floor were kept just burning during the days of winter, and the Doctor could brag how the temperature would hover at about ten degrees centigrade. The classrooms were always especially chilly: here the boys had to sit still on wooden stools during study. There was little help from the two sighted teachers, with so many boys to manage, but the blind boys were not left entirely on their own. Dr. Guillié had introduced the system of *répétiteurs*—another money-saver—in which senior blind students would sit with younger children and help them to learn by touch. It was part of the Director's method of "mutual teaching". The *répétiteurs* would trace the embossed words in the old books, even larger than the original Haüy models, and, parrot-fashion, would repeat and repeat the letters and the words until knowledge was implanted into memory. These so-called coaches gained no special privileges for the service; they ate the same meals at the same tables, slept in the same dormitories, on bunks covered with straw palliasses, but were entitled to a few francs pay each week. It was afterwards known that the Director received some 900 francs a year for this supplementary teaching service; but payment to the senior boys was not equitable. Some were given a few francs each week, some one or two, and some got nothing. (The franc was at the time worth about 20 cents, or eightpence in English money.)

Despite the rigour of the routine, and defying the repressions of the Director, and his obsessions, there was a wonderful spirit in the gloomy institute, as if the example of the patron saint was abroad; for each boy showed devotion to its objective. Hour after hour, young fingers would trace out the letters in the embossed tomes, feeling for the legs of the A, tracing the bow of B, making no confusion between C and G, putting them together as a word, then moving on, word after word, to stitch them in the mind to form sentences of meaning. There was desperate eagerness for learning. Implanted in the consciousness of the pupils was a thirst for knowledge that would stave off the prospect of a useless life, of resort to beggary. There were bonds of common affliction, and companionship flowed freely with competition. It was all so slow, too agonisingly slow, this garnering of knowledge, but it was, oh, so precious!

Frailty was a hindrance to learning, the books of enlarged type, embossed on only one side of the page, were heavy for thin wrists and arms to handle easily. Some subjects would need as many as twenty separate sections, each weighing somewhere around 9 kilograms (20 pounds); and this added to their wearying studies.

Yet these pages could endow their minds with the confidence and capacity to think and act as people who could see—almost. The hunger to learn created a driving force, which swept away tedium; ennui had no place in this tuition of the blind. Fingers were extended to attain unusual sensitivity, hands to greater dexterity, and minds were stretched to grasp and hold facts and knowledge in finely honed memory. There was no recourse to written notes, no pocketbook manuals: there was only assimilation and recall: total, instant, precise. And time was precious, filled with challenge and activity, so that nothing was allowed to dampen eagerness. Discomfort was brushed aside; cold, hunger, no outings, long hours of mental and physical work disregarded, and in that old decaying pile blinded boys and girls surmounted problems and impairment in their seeking of knowledge and capability. So marked was this spirit that Dr. Guillié would turn his thoughts again to the shadow of the saint whose memory lived in the former St-Firmin Seminary, and he would write: "What other place could be more suited to inspiring sentiments of love, service, and charity towards one's fellow human beings than the dwelling of the famous saint who gave his life to bring comfort to suffering mankind?"

Due to his experience with the wild boys brought from the Quinze-Vingt hospice, Dr. Guillié watched all his new charges carefully; so much so, that they were not allowed to leave the building under any circumstance during their first semesters. This meant that in his first months of institutional life Louis Braille would not feel the sun's warmth on his face or the free wind stir his fair hair. The long weeks were spent on assiduous, repetitive study in cold, damp classrooms, breathing an atmosphere heavy with what a future Director would call "foul emanations", each day facing meagre and monotonous meals, drinking a ration of water drawn direct from the Seine, unfiltered and untreated. Malodorous air, polluted water, chill walls of stone on which they could feel the creeping fungus, each day dragooned into strict schedules and implicit obedience, the new boys suffered for knowledge in conditions that would be tolerated for too many years to come. In the classrooms, in the narrow corridor workshops, in the top-floor dormitory, in the covered courtyard and the echoing chapel itself, they lived every hour with the odour of decay in their nostrils. Soon they were to catch the smell of death.

Told secretly, in quiet confidence, they heard the darker side of the history of their building, of the horrific happenings in what the Director had called a "place of silence and prayer". The "evil events", to which he had vaguely referred, became shuddering reality in the minds of the young blind lads. They came to know the horror as the "September Massacre". Blood-chilling details were whispered from bunk to bunk in the quiet hour before sleep, told with bated breath to prevent interference from monitoring *répétiteurs*, details gruesome and lurid enough to fire the imagination. The carnage had happened in the third year of revolution, when Paris was under savage oppression by the fanatics who called themselves the Committee of Public Safety! With nerves stretched by invasion from Austria and Prussia, the revolutionaries used national danger to exert a rule of terror across the land, the infamous *grande peur*. In their campaign of utter brutality they were suddenly gifted with an event to distract the attention of the masses from the nation's predicament.

The inoffensive King Louis XVI and his frivolous queen, Marie Antoinette, fearful of the rise of the Terror in the streets of Paris, had driven north in a carriage with a few royal jewels and a small mounted escort, only to be apprehended and dragged back to face the ruling Committee. Demoniac Robespierre called for their blood as "traitors to the People of France". They would have to meet the kiss of Madame Guillotine. "They must die so that the State can live," he thundered, providing the mob with a circus of royal blood-letting to distract them from the continuing hunger and cold, forgotten when the King and Queen met the dreaded Sanson, public executioner, and their heads dropped into baskets filled with sawdust to soak up the blood. The age of sedate parties, of dancing the minuet and gavotte, of dainty women with hair-dos like frigates in full sail, of lordly men with thin swords dangling from their belts, the Paris of culture that Voltaire and Benjamin Franklin had known, and in which Amadeus Mozart had played, was swept away in a wave of hatred and violence. Angry rhetoric from the "Defenders of the Public Safety" whipped the passions of mobs to a fervour against all former authority, against royalty, nobility and the church, especially against the unarmed, defenceless priesthood.

Bands of vengeful citizens, who viewed wigs and breeches as symbols of past oppression, donned distinctive striped trousers and formed the dreaded *sans culottes*. Their cry of doom echoed through narrow streets, "Death for royalty! Death for the church!"

The wise among the rich fled the land

to safer corners, but there were few bolt-holes for mission-dedicated priests and nuns. Ready for martyrdom, they stayed at their posts until death came roaring down the street, as it did to the old St-Firmin Seminary, in Rue St-Victor, on the first day of September 1792.

Those same oaken doors through which Simon-René Braille had brought his son into the old edifice had been battered open, just as the Bastille had been stormed some three years before. In the gloom of the seminary, however, the killers found more than seven unimportant prisoners to release, and two officials to decapitate. They found a feast for bestiality, rank upon rank of young priests, huddled in terror, some hiding, dozens upon dozens, ready for the slaughter. Yet, this was not mayhem in the bloodlust of the moment. This was methodical extermination, deliberate as it was vicious, inhuman as it was insensible. Steadily over two whole days murder was pursued; on the stairs to the boys' dormitory scores of young Lazarists had been garrotted, stabbed, their bodies butchered and quartered and the remnants thrown from the roof to the courtyard.

In all, some 170 priests were massacred in those two days; a mere handful escaped, and records tell how a later famed naturalist and cleric, Geoffroy St. Hilaire, then a trainee-priest in the Order, decoyed the rabble and led some of his fellows to a ladder he had obtained to climb the wall into an adjoining garden.

To add to wholesale murder there came despoliation. The mob smashed down the door of the room on the first floor that had been sacrosanct since Vincent de Paul's death in 1660. The reverent silence of the room was violated with profanity and destruction. The saint's crucifix, his wooden table and chairs, the cot and straw mat, were thrown into the street to be burned with the holy man's books, amid jeering and derision. The saddened old building was then commandeered by the Committee, and the ugly chapter of its history continued with years of imprisonment, cruelty and eventual debauchery, until the fall of Napoleon in 1815 paved the way for restoration of monarchy and the revival of royal interest in the institute founded by Valentin Haüy.

When the grisly tale was told, covertly,

to the new boys in 1819, less than thirty years had passed since the slaughter; and against the long history of the ancient building the September Massacre would have seemed like yesterday. Sensitive boys could lie tremulous in their bunks, fingering rosaries for comfort, and hear in their minds brutal voices of murderers, thudding of heavy feet on stairways as victims were hunted, death cries echoing through the winding stone passages; and these were sightless boys to whom daylight could not bring bravery. Thus it was fortunate that Dr. Guillié emphasised the exemplar of goodness and humanity in the life of the institute's patron saint, since his voice, too, his footsteps and his prayers in the St-Firmin chapel could also be brought back to life in imagination. Certainly the memory of the saint softened the impact of the macabre massacre and touched the character and mind of the blind boy from Coupvray with the strength of faith. It would be charitable to assume Dr. Guillié's stress on the link with St. Vincent de Paul and his reluctance to detail the "evil events" were out of concern for the morals and mental well-being of his blind charges. But while he was administrator of the institute, he was also a man of medicine, and yet showed no comparable concern for the bodily health of the blind juveniles. His "chubby" children suffered discomfort and restrictions in an environment that a future incumbent of the same post would describe as "miseries of despair". However, nowhere in Dr. Guilliés copious writing on his management is there indication of awareness of the menace of the dreadful conditions in which the young pupils lived, or that their ill-health caused him any anxiety. His reports were expansive expositions of his stewardship, fully detailed on the economic diet, heating measures, how he had checked excesses by staff and reduced consumption of food, wine and fuel; how he had taught blind children to work weaving looms to produce not only textiles for their uniforms but also to sell material to public hospitals for profit. Not once did he register concern at the muddy drinking water, the cold and the damp, or the high rate of illness among the boys and girls.

In most respects Dr. Guillié's picture of the institute's affairs showed an attitude more in keeping with the organisation of a workhouse. Indeed, he would be accused of caring more for money than the welfare of the young blind, and that he never tried to understand the special problems and needs of sightless people. In his defence, Dr. Guillié is seen as a complex man and that in tuition of the pupils he appreciated the need for culture in life.

Guillié had added to the legacy of Valentin Haüy some works in embossed texts considered useless for blind people needing to earn a living in the world of the early nineteenth century. Under Dr. Guillié, students could finger-read in Greek and Latin, study algebra, and learn grammar in Spanish, Italian and English, while prose and poetry were included along with poems, in French, by the great Englishman, John Milton, who wrote *Paradise Lost* and *Paradise Regained* after losing his sight. To practical minds these matters weighed little in preparing the sightless for life, but this view ignores benefits that flow from a broad range of education. The Director reasoned that young blind persons would benefit from a rounding-off of knowledge with some cultural activity. Art requiring vital co-ordination of hand and eye, painting, sculpture, architecture, even staging of opera, could not be reached from a lifelong prison of darkness. Not so other cultural subjects, creative literature, poetry, drama, and his own special interest—music!

No records exist of what was spent to form an orchestra from the talent at the institute. The Director used all means he could to obtain instruments—violins, cellos, double-bass, piano—and he also had a small organ installed in the chapel. He gained the interest of sighted pro-fessional musicians in Paris, who made regular teaching visits, and, refusing to allow this to be a matter of whim for the pupils, he made the subject of music compulsory. This was a gift of enchant-ment to the blind boy from the village of Coupvray. Before he was twelve years old, Louis Braille discovered new joys of sound, glorious music, quite beyond his rustic upbringing, and a natural aptitude that brought him confidence-building ability as well as a lifelong companionship with another blind boy with a bent for music, Gabriel Gauthier. Both were immediately fascinated with this new-found delight, though they had yet to find their way to music through written works.

Dr. Guillié's approach to teaching was very basic. It was another avenue of his "mutual teaching", though even in this milieu he cut costs. Outside musicians gave their time freely; and for rehearsing musical passages, *répétiteurs* filled the role, repeating and repeating phrases and set pieces, to brand them into memory. Dr. Guillié achieved an ambition, to train the first orchestra of blind juveniles; but everything they performed, solo or in unison, had to be learned by rote, and produced *par coeur*.

No consideration was given to the possibility that imposed repetition would breed resistance and boredom among the less musically inclined; for Louis Braille and Gabriel Gauthier, however, nothing could dull the delight of their new enchantment. And when Simon-René came again to the institute to take his son home for the summer vacation, the boy had two new joys in his world: music and his musical friend.

Nicolas-Marie Charles Barbier de la Serre, Captain of Artillery in the forces of Emperor Napoleon, was a prickly, difficult man. He was adjudged to be withdrawn, of sad disposition, but was also a fount of fertile ideas. In that summer of 1819, when Louis Braille rode with his father in the stage coach from Paris to Meaux for the first vacation at Coupvray, the morose Captain had already fired the opening shot that would lead to benefaction for the world's blind people. He, like all others involved in the Braille epic, would never live to know the full implications.

The Captain was a product of four generations of French nobility. Son of the Keeper of the King's Estates, he had been born at Valenciennes in May 1767, and by virtue of his class was allotted a place at the age of fifteen in the royal college of artillery, a training ground for élite, stiff-backed officers of utter loyalty to the Bourbon monarchy. By the time he was twenty-two, French blood had been spilled on the cobbles of Paris, the Bastille had been stormed, and the juggernaut of revolutionary Terror had begun to roll. Like many young men from notable families, he became an *émigré*, escaping to the sudden attraction of North America, where, it was reported, he lived for a time with a Red Indian tribe still with French affiliation, and then worked as a surveyor. When France emerged into the imperialism of Napoleon and had new need of soldiers, he returned to serve under the colours, though, with the thin veneer of revolutionary democracy that was abroad, he dropped his appellations of noble breeding and became plain Captain Charles Barbier.

In his experience of battle in the Napoleonic Wars the Captain had known of a forward gunpost being over-run and the men slaughtered when they betrayed their position by lighting a lamp to read night orders from headquarters. The loss of good men fired the Captain's fertile mind, and he began to cast around for a method of framing orders in a form that would need neither light, nor eyes, but which could be deciphered by touch, in the dark. From this concentration of thought the Artillery Captain came up with his notion of "cut writing". His proposal dispensed with quill and nibs, and instead used a pen-knife! With a configuration of cuts and bumps, and all could be prepared in triplicate or more at the same time with the same knife, he formed rough symbols for phonetic sounds, which could be interpreted by the reading fingers of trained people.

The method was too crude, however, and so Captain Barbier began to build complexity into his system, using a blunt-nosed stylus to effect a pattern of raised bumps and strokes with which he could indicate a variety of sounds and numerals. The generals were unimpressed. With typical military suspicion of anything new —perhaps not concerned with the trivia of forward posts being over-run, or even finding the Captain's code too complex for simple soldierly minds—they decided Charles Barbier's notion should expire in a dusty pigeon-hole. But it took more than high-level lack of interest to quench the fire of invention in Charles Barbier. The aristocratic Captain was nothing if not tenacious; and it is easy now to vision his response to rebuff: chin jutting, moustache bristling with defiance, refusing to desert his inspiration.

Throughout some of the most climactic years in French history—the débâcle of the retreat from Moscow, Napoleon's exile to Elba, the fiasco of the Hundred Days, the battle of Waterloo, the second restoration of King Louis XVIII—the undefeated Captain worked on improving his code of dots and impressions. He devised a long grooved ruler, with a sliding guide, to impress his symbols into thin cardboard, to shut his signs into squares and confine them to six lines. On and on, through the dramatic years he worked, until by summer of 1819 he had reached a polished system, which he named *écriture nocturne*. And still, as implied by the title of "night writing", his sights were set on eventual use as a method of communication for commanders in the field of battle. These were easier times for the Captain, now in his mid-fifties. A new situation in officialdom had come with the return of the monarchy, and former *émigrés* from families of the *ancien régime* were competing for important posts and promotions citing the strength of their ancestry and loyalty to the crown. Captain Barbier felt the time ripe in mid–1819 to seek an influential nod of approval for his system of "night writing" from the most respected scientific body in the land.

Through the Institut de France he won a concession; it was agreed that a panel from the Academy of Sciences should hear details of his proposed writing system. On 28 June, that year of 1819, he stood to recount the results of his long efforts in the same interviewing room where, some thirty-five years earlier, Valentin Haüy had outlined his work among blind children and won approval that went on to earn the warmth of a royal smile. There was no such immediate outcome for Captain Barbier. He was heard courteously by the eminent scientists, his ingenuity was praised (though not his originality), and no action was recommended. Almost a year later, in the following May, when the report of the panel appeared in the Academy's printed notes, it caused not a ripple of interest. Barbier's *écriture nocturne* seemed to have sunk without trace.

By the time Captain Charles Barbier

read the noncommittal report on his code of raised dots, Louis Braille was completing his first full year at the institute for blind juveniles. His return from vacation to the old seminary building held none of the uncertainty and inner quaking that he felt when he first came with his father. This time there was no frowning perusal by a brooding Director; Louis Braille now belonged; he was part of institutional life. He could distinguish between echoes in the curving stone corridors, knew where to locate workshops, classrooms, refectory and stairs, and could put his fingers on the piano in the common room. He did not know that this room had an opening in the wall through which Dr. Guillié could secretly see his charges and monitor their behaviour.

When, in 1820, the weeks were drawing towards the time when he would ride home again in the stage coach, Louis was already proving an exceptional student. He was awarded the first of many prizes. It was a joint award, for progress in French grammar and skilled handcraft, and hardly another year would pass in his formative education when his name would be missing from the annual prize lists. This first recognition came from the long days of study in which he had a head start from skill gained from the dogged patience of his artisan father. Persistence in those early years of blindness, running infant fingertips across the crude alphabet boards, had endowed a priceless sensitivity of instant recognition. As with muscle and sinew, and tissues of the brain, constant use of the touch receptor cells in his fingertips had developed a remarkable facility to inform an alert mind no longer distracted by even a scintilla of light. This ultra-sensitive channel of communication was matched by concentration that fastened fact into memory.

Perversely, rising into his teens, the gift claimed a price in frustration. Oral teaching was sparse, coming only from the limited knowledge of the *répétiteur* students or in the snatches of time the over-pressed teachers could spare. The main source of information was wrested from the heavy embossed tomes, and, as the months went by, with his increasing expertise, feeling for individual letters to form single words was excruciatingly slow.

Learning came at too glacial a speed for the emerging mind of Louis Braille. His burgeoning genius was seeking a more distant horizon of knowledge than was offered in these facilities. At twelve years of age the boy felt a need for wider scope, for quicker methods to satisfy his hunger for knowledge, something to help surmount the barrier of his impairment. The yearning was obvious to other blinded pupils. One of them was to note how "Braille always tried to break out of his cage of darkness".

In those long days of study was born the aching need for a speedier pathway, a way to circumvent the bottleneck of the cumbersome books. Yet nowhere in the writings of the Director at this time is there a note of awareness of this unusual pupil. The only record Dr. Guillié was to make of this lively intellect was the original entry of admission to the institute, on 15 February 1819, of the boy from the Commune of Coupvray. But there was excuse for the omission; the Director's supervising powers in those critical months had been dulled by other attractions, not then known to the blind students. Very soon, however, a scandal of infatuation and indiscretion broke the routine of the institute, and official indifference burst into sudden awareness that would not only alter the tone of the establishment, but also would enhance prospects for the twelve-year-old Louis Braille.

Changing seasons of the year had meant little more to the inmates of the Institut Royale des Jeunes Aveugles than changes in temperature. Cold was winter and time to warm chilled fingers near the smouldering stoves; summer was hot and brought the only time when the daily schedule was put aside; Easter and Christmas, apart from special religious services, brought no break in the strict routine. Change came only that one time in August, when those pupils lucky enough to be able to travel home were taken off by relatives.

Not so in the early months of 1821. Spring that year brought a change in the pattern of strictly controlled activity. It brought a fresh approach to the process of learning, a new effort at understanding and caring for the needs of the blind; and a refreshing aura of good will between authority and pupils. The severe, unbending taskmaster was replaced by a father figure, by the first man to recognise and record the promise of talent in the pupil who would open doors for blind people of the world.

Indications of change had been noticed by the few sighted boys, and innuendoes had been whispered behind the backs of the *répétiteurs*. Their eyes had made connection between sardonic remarks by sighted teachers (based on the Molière play, *L'Amour medecin*) and the changing shape of a young lady teacher, whom Dr. Guillié had selected for employment at the institute. There had been giggles about strict segregation between the two sections of the institute when the coming and going from the Director's private quarters had been noticed.

Boyish gossip in dark dormitories was harmless, but facts were straws in the wind that made ammunition for members of the staff with little respect for the "amorous doctor", and subordinate sniping soon ensured that information was passed on to the aristocratic Count Alexis de Noailles.

Within the normal pattern of French morality of the time, few would see offence in the Director having his own salacious side-interest. After all, a mistress was a mistress, and no bad thing! Indeed, in many cases, expectations of a man of power and substance and vitality would be that he should keep a beautiful woman content other than the lady of his ménage. Why, even the ageing King Louis had Zoë, the so-called Countess of Cayla, a witty, luscious woman of some twenty-odd years, who was separated from an "unworthy spouse". She was ensconced in the royal apartment on regular occasions, it was blandly claimed, for the purpose of playing chess with the old monarch, games requiring such remarkable concentration that not only did the King lock the doors, but he had them guarded against all intrusion. And nobody would think of sacking the King. Such things were accepted. Even Napoleon, despite all his warring, had found time to keep a mistress or two.

But the *affaire* at the institute for blind children could not be ignored, nor condoned under the umbrella of fashionable morality. Once the matter was brought to the Count's personal notice (the King's predilication for chess notwithstanding) the liaison in the former historic seminary was condemned as an outrage. Not only had the Doctor been entrusted with the bodily and moral health of the blind children, but so had his paramour! It was a scandal that affronted the Count, who at once sought the opinion of his fellow members of the governing committee, the band of eminent citizens, nobles and select executives from the Ministry. And, with the fading royal interest in mind, they decided that both the Director and the lady teacher should vanish from the scene at the institute and be replaced by a more reliable and suitable person.

It was a revealing reaction. It showed Dr. Guillié was not alone in placing the moral health of his charges above bodily well-being, that there was no more concern in the governing committee for the dangerously insanitary conditions in which they kept the selected blind children of France than there had been in the Director himself. Not until the Count and his coterie had themselves been swept away would consideration be given to housing the sightless juveniles in healthier surroundings. But, by then, it would be too late for some of the pupils Dr. Guillié left behind.

When Dr. André Pignier strode into the old building on Rue St-Victor to take up his custodianship, it was little more than two years since Simon-René Braille brought his son to the institute for blind juveniles. The new Director had every reason to be shocked by what he found behind the double oaken doors. When Dr. Guillié had brought his band of unruly blind pupils here in 1815, to the age-old home for destitute children, sometime Lazarite seminary, guard house, whorehouse and prison, he had found the place acceptable. Dr. Pignier had been serving for many years as doctor-in-charge of welfare at a modern and well-endowed seminary, St-Sulpice, and he could never find the dilapidated building acceptable.

From his first day at the Institut Royale des Jeunes Aveugles Dr. Pignier would commit himself to winning a different venue. On that late winter day he came face to face with the reality of Dr. Guillié's dereliction of duty as a physician. He saw conditions and a pattern of hard life within the decaying walls.

For a caring man of medicine, it was a tempering experience, to tread groaning staircases, see dark stone-flanked corridors where sightless children worked with faces to the wall; to stand in cold rooms where young fingers traced letters in big books; to see baskets, carpets and slippers being stitched together with only a tarpaulin for shelter against snowy skies; to hear the factory-like clatter of looms churning out cloth; and everywhere, over all, the smell of wet decay, condensation dribbling down grimy walls, and the pungency of verdant mildew.

Dismay, shock, whatever Dr. Pignier felt on his initial survey of his new domain, he had yet to make a close inspection of the inmates. He was a sturdy, determined man, but was warm-hearted enough to be appalled at what he found. Blind youngsters whom Dr. Guillié had described in his reports to the Ministry as "chubby" were paraded in the assembly room, and they stood in lines with wan faces turned upwards, or sideways, to catch the voice of the new Director, faces that had not seen sunshine for months, features that seemed even more sallow above the drab blue calico uniforms drawn tight over thin bodies by a single front row of brass buttons. They held their hands together in front, with fingers entwined, a sign of submission in the presence of high authority, and they could not keep still, someone was always coughing.

The new Director was moved by a scene he would not forget; from that first day he was committed to the cause of the blind in a dedication that would go on beyond his two decades of service in the institute. He resolved he would not rest until these sightless young people were in a new home, instead of languishing in a relic of antiquity. Dr. Pignier would be described by others, who coveted his role, as pious, too liberal, too easy with pupils; but with his commitment to change conditions for the young blind persons, he would always have a claim on the gratitude of those that followed—on Braille, on Gauthier, on the many remarkable young people who passed through at the institute in subsequent decades.

Lacking the egocentricity of Dr. Guillié, the new Director, a man of culture and conscience, was a realist. He had to be to succeed; for from the start of his term in the office as head of the institute he faced the prospect of moving a mountain of indifference. And if he was easy on some of his pupils, the reward came in the blossoming of the latent genius of Louis Braille, which can be counted as one of Dr. Pignier's triumphs. From his first weeks on Rue St-Victor he made changes to the lifestyle of the inmates. He saw clearly that sighted people, no matter the depth of their compassion and sympathy, *could not* truly understand what it meant to live in a world of total darkness, to be dependent on the senses of touch, hearing, taste and smell. He knew the institute was governed by sighted men, leading the blind blindly. He soon perceived how the people who controlled the purse-strings had salved their consciences with the fallacious argument that since the blind boys and girls could not see the filth and the slimy walls, they did not exist for them. Dr. Pignier would not wipe from his mind the picture of the children lined before him in the dim assembly hall with their burning hope for some chance of a better life, and the threat of ill-health hanging over their heads.

It was not long before Dr. Pignier reached the conclusion that he could not move the mountain on his own; there had to be help from outside. He would open the institute to the world, and he would open something of the outside world to his pupils. Without any link ever being made in his time, he led the institute along the same path that Valentin Haüy had followed in the years before the Terror. Both worked to bring the blind into the age of enlightenment and, very soon, fortuitously, they would be brought together.

The first months of the Pignier régime were heavy with coincidence and with portent. Two of the new Director's initial decisions were crucial to all that would follow. He realised that touching the hearts and minds of decision-makers in the remote rooms of the Ministry of the Interior would be a hard task, especially if he had to work through the aristocratic Count and his apathetic committee. Some shock had to be administered. He had contacts in the professions from his former work; he had powerful friends in the church and in medicine. He decided to use first an appeal to conscience and to patriotism. This institute was the first of its kind in the world, a French innovation, but its subjects were being grossly neglected, perilously so. The danger to the health of the blind children was a national responsibility. There he would strike his first blow.

Two eminent consultants from the Paris Faculty of Medicine lent their names and prestige to his original move. On a bright spring day in May 1821 they arrived at the institute to see for themselves a situation disturbing and outrageous. Professors Récaimer and Cayol stayed much longer than they intended; they studied conditions and examined and talked with every boy and every girl; they worked through the hours until the oil lamps were lit. They went away in the dark of night, troubled, and wrote their report:

The first thing that struck us was the appearance of these young unfortunates. Their pale faces, their thin bodies, suggested that most of them were diseased and consumptive. We found swollen glands, ganglions in a number of throats, and signs of scrofula, or a morbid condition, while many children have digestive complaints—especially among the girls—from a malady we suspect is rare among adolescents. We attribute much of this to the building and its location. The institute is in a low-lying situation, is poorly ventilated, and subject to putrid emanations; the ground floor is especially damp and cold, while what open areas there are are wet underfoot. The infirmary, which should be the healthiest place in an institute for young people, is totally unsuited to this function. It has two tiny windows, wrongly placed for replenishing fresh air; and it lacks all things essential for care of the sick. These are only general comments, and we reserve a more detailed opinion for a further report should this prove to be necessary. Signed, Récaimer and Cayol, May 1821.

Dr. Pignier lost that first battle, and further reports and his exposé of the situation for the selected blind children of France would have to continue. The plight of the sightless was water on bureaucratic backs. There were men in influential posts who had been young and ambitious during the Empire, and whose eyes and minds were fixed on the current uncertainty of the government under the Duc de Richelieu, on reports of outbreaks of revolution in corners of the land and even in some of the regiments of the line. And the old King's power was quickly waning. With prospects of opportunities for quick advancement in sudden change, who could give thought to the situation of a few dozen blind children? But Dr. Pignier was a persistent man as well as a realist; lack of interest in the Ministry, lack of concern in the Count's little clique, would not halt other plans he had in mind for the betterment of his charges. He introduced changes to the curriculum and the pattern of life for the young pupils; he brought in outside volunteer helpers, including his sister, who taught carpet weaving, knitting and basket-making, and he enlisted the aid and the interest of the Order St. Vincent de Paul had founded, all of which were to be added to by the adventure of outside excursions.

The first of these outings was to be known as the "rope-walk". This innovation was aimed at new horizons of interest for the young pupils and at getting fresh air into their lungs. These were weekly outings with a sighted teacher in the lead and a dozen or so youngsters clutching a length of rope with one hand. There was individual joy in this release from the grim building, to shamble out of the Rue St-Victor and past the boundary of the Paris Faculty to the Jardin des Plantes, to catch the sweet scent of grass and hear birdsong in the trees, with the teacher at the head of the rope telling of the colours of flowers and shrubs, and sometimes taking them into the famed Museum of Natural Sciences that stood in a corner of the Botanical Gardens.

There was a tenuous contact with coming history in this building, with the curator of geological specimens speaking with the students, allowing them to feel a collection of rock samples that intrigued that man because, he told them, they glowed in the dark. The curator was Dr. César Becquerel, whose grandson, Henri, would win fame as the first human being to detect radiation from uranium, from one of the samples collected by his grandfather. This was a finding that led to the discovery—also in Paris—of two new elements, radium and polonium, by a young woman doctoral student from Poland, who would be known later as Marie Curie.

There was a more direct link between the museum and the institute. One of the small apartments allocated to workers in special fields was occupied by a leader in the emerging science of crystallography, the Abbé René-Just Haüy, who had been held in the old building in Rue St-Victor when the revolutionaries used it as a prison. The connection was even stronger; the Abbé's brother, M. Valentin Haüy, shared the apartment with him and had done so for the last five years, ever since he had returned from his exile in Russia. He had chosen to live with his brother so as to be close to the institute he had founded, only to face heartless exclusion.

For five years he had sat out his days in the little flat overlooking the gardens, neglected for his past role—indeed, deliberately ignored—and unhonoured. He was now seventy-six years old, the prime of his life spent in service to the blind, the first great benefactor, and he sat each day in loneliness in the museum apartment.

In that summer of 1821, Dr. Pignier learned of the old man's whereabouts; and if Valentin Haüy felt bitterness, or simmering anger, it would all vanish in a surge of delight and recognition from the Director's spontaneous humanity.

At the time of the annual ceremony of awarding prizes among the best of the institute pupils, the Director sent a carriage to bring the Founder back into the institute. Staff and students, informed of the history of the institute, stood in welcoming lines and applauded as the stooping figure entered the assembly hall. Dr. Pignier planned carefully for the return of Valentin Haüy. He had found a song of gratitude, written by some of the first blind pupils back in the year 1788, just before the revolution. Then, in their own home as a private institution, pupils of that time had, in their gratitude, written a musical tribute, which they had sung to their Founder, fittingly, on St. Valentine's Day. Dr. Pignier revived this treasured moment for the lonely old man, he winnowed the best voices from the pupils and thoroughly rehearsed them until they were perfect in memory and harmony.

So it came about that on 21 August 1821, the day of Valentin Haüy's belated reunion with the establishment he had founded, he heard again the song first sung to him in the last year of the *ancien régime*. Coming back across a half a lifetime, after a third of a century, the voices of the young blind would have sounded like a choir of angels in his ears.

Renewed affection in his failing days touched the old man deeply; it is known how, wet-eyed, he walked among the pupils, taking their hands in his and speaking his love, and his gratitude. There is no specific record that Louis Braille was a member of the choir, though it is likely because of his musical gifts. Imagination allows the thought that at some time on that day of joy the hand of the Founder and the inventor of the system of embossed reading would have touched the hand of the boy whose life's work would endow the world's blind with their own alphabet. What is on record is that the twelve-year-old boy felt love and thankful respect for the old man; for when the news reached the institute, only a month after the next Saint Valentine's Day, that Valentin Haüy had died, Louis Braille broke into tears.

One day in the spring of that same year the light of inspiration shone on the gloomy hopes of Captain Charles Barbier. Through some agency, never disclosed, it dawned on his military mind that the system of raised dots he'd advocated to the army, and which had been ignored, might have a useful future among people with impaired sight. The Captain wasted no time, but wrote—going directly to the top —asking the Count de Noailles for an interview. The noble-minded Count sat in his office on the morning of 11 April 1821, and listened enthralled to details of the *écriture nocturne* code and saw how it could be supremely useful for the blind. Two sighted men, they both enthused at the prospect; they saw no barrier for the reading fingers at the institute, and the Count undertook to raise the proposal with his committee and to give it his own strong backing.

A week later the Captain knew the first thrill of acceptance of the code that had no need of eyes. The Count's letter of enthusiasm was a reward for the years of frustrations: "We think your discovery first-rate. We have great expectation of your invention; and we have no doubt that you will be esteemed as a benefactor of those unfortunate persons we strive to integrate into normal society . . ." And more, the Count thought the name of Charles Barbier would be linked with those of men of such stature as Valentin Haüy.

The captain's *écriture nocturne* still had to be evaluated, not by sighted enthusiasts, but by the blind themselves. Charles Barbier called on Dr. Pignier in the Rue St-Victor and joined in discussion on size and type of material considered most suitable. Thereafter he began weeks of patient preparation, converting the system from night use by the military to that needed by blind students. He worked with a grooved ruler in which the lines ran longitudinally, over which two sliding clips formed a grille (or *agrafe*) to make a "window" over a sheet of thin cardboard. Through this "window" he used a blunted stylus to make impressions that became raised dots on the opposite side of the thin cardboard. Thus, working always in reverse, he fashioned his patterns, each contained within its own "window", which carried the intelligence. With twelve dots in two columns, starting with two at the top and changing by steps to a dozen in two vertical lines, he could represent thirty-six sounds—vowels, syllables and consonants—and, with the use of other symbols, give a range of numbers. He offered direct coded expression to replace the ponderous finger-reading of the Haüy-style tomes.

In the last weeks before the summer vacation, Director Pignier pondered the tests that would be made with the dotted cards from Captain Barbier. Evaluation needed to be balanced, not the assessment of sighted teachers, nor just opinion from the top one or two of the senior blind pupils; he decided to get reaction from a cross-section of the institute, including the younger students. And it was here that the record of Louis Braille came to his mind. In the awards, made on points allotted by teachers, the name of the boy from the village of Coupvray had been called four times. He was only twelve years old, but he took the top prize for geography and the sole prize for debate; the first prize for French grammar also carried his name; and—showing his rapid advance in musical capacity—he won the sole award for mastery of the cello, defeating the efforts of his friend Gabriel Gauthier.

Dr. Pignier made a special point of speaking with this outstanding pupil, and so began an association that strengthened over the years. The Director sought to explore the capacity of the boy's mind, to feel for balanced judgement, or detect whether the scholastic record was just performance of superb recall. He was surprised at the intellect in one so young. He recorded how he found, behind the outward manner of quiet reserve, there was "a rectitude of mind and a clarity of ideas".

From this meeting the Director wrote

the first contemporary description of the adolescent Louis Braille: "He made a distinct impression with his gentle intelligence and his great facility of mind. On his fine features one could see a certain childish gravity, an expression of serenity of mind, and human kindness."

To this vignette the Director added his own reaction to the swift, brilliant smile that years before had captured the hearts of the Braille family and their friends: "There would be rare times in our conversation when his face would suddenly light up in a radiant smile, with a vivacity and animation that contrasted beautifully with his normal calm expression."

In this first exchange with the blind youth Dr. Pignier reached inspired decision. Louis Braille was among the young pupils selected to test the usefulness of Captain Barbier's columns of raised dots and bars. The device went home with him in the Meaux stage coach that summer of 1823, seemingly a toy for his fingertips to play with and his mind to explore during quiet days in the Brie village.

4

The Domino Six

IT was the autumn of 1821. The caterpillars of blind pupils were again on their rope-walk excursions to the Jardin des Plantes. Mellow sun on their faces, feet scuffing fallen leaves, hands clutching the linking backbone of rope, they moved again under the window of the man who had bequeathed them their method of reading. Now, however, with but a few months of life left to benefactor Valentin Haüy, there was a new, indeed exciting, prospect of access to information. Students fortunate enough to have gone home for the summer vacation, and those who stayed at the institute, had lavished spare hours on the dotted cards and ruled boards that the Captain of Artillery had deposited with Director Pignier before the summer break. In the ensuing months the boys had responded strongly to the challenge. The new system was unfamiliar and demanding. They had been trained to read the embossed Haüy-style books, tracing letters into words, words into sentences of meaning. Here, under their exploring fingertips, they had to find a new mastery; they had to decipher arrangements of dots within two vertical columns, to seek symbols to indicate when numbers were intended, to sound the syllables in the mind to reach passages of meaning.

It was a patience-testing process, but it was new and exciting. It opened another access to information, which promised to be speedier than reading raised letters of the alphabet, and more than just a promise of relief from the tedium of stitching vowels into consonants to find words that formed sentences. It offered a prospect of being able to make notes during lessons for study after hours. For the first time, the blind pupils were offered a method of communication between themselves that could be utterly private. They enthused over these offerings as they struggled to become familiar with symbolic arrangements of dots in vertical columns.

The enthusiasm, the dedication to mastery of the Captain's code, delighted the Director. He had been courageous. He had broken with tradition in allowing the blind *to evaluate for themselves* what seemed best, rather than leave judgement, as hitherto, in the province of sighted members of the governing committee. He had erected a milestone in the hope and expectation that the Barbier code was an advance of the highest importance, as critical for the sightless as Valentin Haüy's texts in relief had been. And in the first flush of that anticipation he wrote, glowingly, to the Captain:

I am certain that you will be delighted to know with what enthusiasm your code of night writing has been received at this institute. Our boys are back from the summer vacation most eager to put your system into daily practice. I am hopeful that one day, soon, you will be able to visit us when I can show you results that you will not find disappointing . . .

Dr. Pignier's letter brought a taste of success to Captain Charles Barbier. At long last, it seemed, there was a home for his carefully refined, long-nurtured creation, the conception that had occupied the prime years of his life. And more heart-warming than this was that his system would prove helpful to unfortunates who had lost their sight. Military indifference to his inspiration and the struggle for recognition were behind him, and now he waited with soldierly patience for the time to arrive when he would see his brainchild come alive under the fingers of the pupils in the Paris institute for the young blind.

Winter days grew short. In dark December cold fingers were warmed at pot-bellied stoves; rope-walks in the gardens were cancelled to wait for more clement weather, and so spare hours saw intense and critical examination of the Barbier code of reading. Before the year was out, the limitations had been exposed. From the first days the Captain's title for his system was rejected. Young people whose lives were spent in total blackness could not accept "night writing" as apt. They changed the name to Sonography, or sometimes Stenography, which they found more fitting. The method, devised for soldiers reading orders in the dark of night, emerged as just a form of shorthand in sound. True, it could be used to transmit information faster than reading separate letters of the alphabet. True, it made note-taking and private communication possible, but it did not, could not, *educate*! It was phonetic; and for Barbier's code to begin to make sense in the mind, formal knowledge of language and its structure were first needed. This was only one limitation of a code devised by a man with sight for people who could not see. Sonography gave no aid to spelling, to composition or essay-writing, was no use in grammar, or geography, and, so, was nothing more than an adjunct to learning reached with raised texts.

Pupils, teachers, and Director, all brought to this realisation, felt let down; and so, when the Captain of Artillery came to see the transformation his inspiration had wrought with the teaching methods at the Paris institute, the disappointment was general and easily marked. His beloved *écriture nocturne* was now Sonography, and a side-issue. Dr. Pignier had produced no tomes of study; there were no instruction manuals based on his vertical columns of raised dots. He saw at once that no special arrangements had been made to install his system as part of the curriculum of teaching. Individual students happily demonstrated their new facility with ruled board, stylus and the thin cardboard he had supplied, but—though they were surprisingly adept—there was none of the enthusiasm indicated in the Director's earlier correspondence. The Captain, however, did talk with some of the practitioners of his code, and it is recorded that among them was the lad from the village of Coupvray.

In hindsight, this meeting is intriguing. However, it must have seemed then to the Captain, the aristocratic officer, proud and untouched by modesty, matching wits with the blind lad just into his teens, pale, thin, self-effacing, respectful, quietly mannered, but critical, gently indicating that there were shortcomings to the system. The code was phonetic, with symbols to represent sound; and was without punctuation—no commas, no semi-colons, no full stops, accents, or apostrophes—so that symbolised sounds ran on in the mind, one into another, and became chaotic, and jumbled meaning. Being phonetic condemned the Captain's vertical columns to restricted use, though, it might be suggested, with respect, that further study could produce changes, alterations that would widen its use by blind people.

If Captain Charles Barbier de la Serre bridled at his first meeting with the precocious intellect that would put his name into history, he would have been so entitled, but nothing is known of his reaction at the time. However, his subsequent actions showed he clung to the belief that he was right and the blind students were wrong. In due time, however, with generosity and grace, he would pay tribute in acknowledging the capacity of the boy named Louis Braille.

The winter of 1821–22 was the winter of Sonography; for the inmates of the Paris institution there were other events to shape the future. Out of Dr. Pignier's vow to open the institute to the world and the world to the blind juveniles came benefits of spiritual uplift, exaltation and new horizons, when priests from the nearby church of St-Nicolas-du-Chardonnet instructed eligible students to prepare them for confirmation. Both Gabriel Gauthier and Louis Braille were instructed. For the lad from Coupvray the preparation and instruction, the service and ritual induction into the embrace of the Mother Church was nourishment of soul and spirit, building as it did on tenets of faith sown in his mind during his early years of blindness by the curé of his village, the former Benedictine monk, Father Palluy. As well, there was the gift of liturgical music, choir and organ, to knit even closer the relationship between the two lads, a bond strengthened by respect and admiration for each other's gifts.

The old church, straggling in wooden-faced ugliness just off dusty, busy St-Germain, became for both boys a place of beauty and delight, where, when the day came, they could sit at the organ and cull from the old pipes chords of *written* music. This joy came to them from another opportunity, which marked the early months of that same year, a new resource to music, magnetic in its appeal to young minds ever yearning for new knowledge and closer contact with culture.

It came as a final legacy from the founder of the institute, even as Valentin Haüy lay dying in the small apartment in the museum in Jardin des Plantes. Somehow, sorrow at the death of their benefactor made even sweeter their new discovery, a book of impressed musical scores, which had, by marvellous fortune, escaped wanton destruction, to reappear in the curriculum of the institute.

Probably the first book of music ever to have been impressed in relief, simple melodies and plain chant, songs and airs, with the notation raised on thick paper and the sheets stuck together, it was a tome that would earn a place both in the history of France and among the blind people of the world. Its origin was in the old Foire St-Ovide, on that September Sunday half a century earlier, when the young civil servant had been repelled by insults and abuse hurled at inoffensive blind men and boys used as a comical, makeshift orchestra. The impression left by that event fed the inspiration to have the book produced, in that last year of the *ancien régime*, before the storming of the Bastille, so that Valentin Haüy's blind pupils could have knowledge of the form and structure of written music. It had gone with the pupils into the home for deaf and dumb children, had somehow been preserved during the "mournful years", when Napoleon committed the institute to the Quinze-Vingt horror; it had been smuggled out when Dr. Guillié lifted the best of the blind children into the ancient pile on Rue St-Victor, and then it had lain, ignored, for a further six years.

Director Pignier did not feel that recognition of the work of Valentin Haüy might lessen his own authority. Instead, he held that the Founder's role added a unifying spirit among the blind inmates of the institution. He allowed the book of impressed sheets of music to go under the fingers of the best students. To days of feeling their way along slimy walls, to weeks of monotonous diet, sleeping in the cold, dank dormitory, Dr. Pignier added a wonderland for them to explore. In the Founder's book, raised for the touch, was written music, as taught to people with sight! To the sounds of notes, chords, and descant, the blind pupils could find instructive notation—staves, breve, semi-breve, minim, crochet and quaver. Music by ear had shape, new meaning, a wider form, and for Gabriel Gauthier and Louis Braille there was a new horizon in their darkened world. Music was a rich subject, and ahead was familiarity with powerful and beautiful new compositions sweeping the concert halls of Europe—from Mozart, Beethoven and Franz Joseph Haydn—Haydn especially for Louis Braille, for the master had died in the year Braille was born and much of his work was dedicated to the glory of God.

Challenge and wonderment graced their hours in the music room, or at the chapel organ. And new zest came from another of Dr. Pignier's innovations. Special teachers attended music lessons. Madame Van Der Burgh, noted piano teacher, spent many hours with Gauthier and Braille as they bent their heads over the keys seeking notes by touch; the organist from Notre-Dame, Dr. Marigues, gave guidance in the chapel; and from the Paris Conservatorium, string-instrument virtuoso Bénazet taught mastery and emotional skill on the cello. These were services that brought reward, for one boy recognition as a composer of talent, for another the role of organist in leading churches of Paris and the gift of teaching that would help other students in future years, even sighted pupils.

Once again Director Pignier was able to open avenues of study and experience of the outside world to his best pupils. Through years of pious service with the St-Sulpice Seminary he had friends and contacts in the Lazarite movement (that St. Vincent de Paul had founded), and through these was able to arrange for his most promising young organists to have turns of a month or so playing in well-known churches for Sunday services. Among these churches were St-Etienne-du-Mont, St-Médard and— most particularly for Louis Braille— St-Nicolas-des-Champs.

In this special church the young musician found associations with the memory of the patron saint of the institute and world patron saint of charity, Vincent de Paul. The great humanist had attended this church when he was tutor and chaplain to the family of the powerful Archbishop Gondi of Paris. It was believed that Vincent de Paul had a hand in the building of the organ in 1632, the very year he moved from the building in Rue St-Victor to the Priory at St. Lazare. And just beneath where Louis Braille sat at the old organ, a revelation at Pentecost in 1623 had inspired Louise de Marillac to found the Order of the Sisters of Charity under the direction of Vincent, which eventually led to her being canonised in 1945 and declared (by Pope John, in 1960) as universal patron of social services. For Louis Braille it seemed there had been a protecting hand held over this old church in the years of the Terror, when a maddened mob came to pillage and burn, but were diverted by the organist of the day thundering out the notes of the Marseillaise. Though quick thinking had saved the church from destruction, it had nevertheless been converted to a revolutionary "temple of marriage". These were memories the blind teenage organist could evoke each time he drew chords from the ancient instrument; and, over all, was the recollection of the devotions here of St.

Vincent de Paul. Each time Louis Braille heard mass, each July in the institute when the commemorative service was held for the patron saint, the spirit of the man became a living presence in his mind, and from this he drew comfort and guidance in the years ahead.

Captain Nicolas-Marie Charles Barbier de la Serre was undeterred. Inventor of the raised dot phonetic code, he remained stubbornly convinced of the value of his "night writing": he was right, the blind students were wrong, and he would prove it. In the months subsequent to his disappointing visit to the old building on Rue St-Victor and his meeting with young Louis Braille, Barbier's attitude firmed even more, almost defiantly. Where before he had described his system as an "aid to the blind", he now pronounced it to be the "final solution to the problem of reading by the blind". Yet for Captain Barbier, as with Braille and Gauthier, this was a period of some diversion, and as the year of 1823 moved on, he had second thoughts on the democratic foreshortening of his name to plain Charles Barbier.

The times had brought changes in the importance of rank in public life. Following the restoration of the Bourbon monarchy, titled backgrounds had new currency, in the strict sense. Some 70,000 *émigrés*, such as he, who had fled the Terror and had lost holdings by confiscation, were to be indemnified by act of Parliament, and hundreds of millions of francs would be involved in the payout. As well, men of noted families who had returned to public life were doing exceptionally well. There was Chateaubriand, writer and orator, and now politician raised to ministerial rank. There was Victor Hugo, son of a Napoleonic general, who had found an aristocratic line back in his family tree. The King had admired the writing talent of the young Hugo and had awarded him a pension of a thousand francs a year to enable further development of his gifts. Talent for invention, the Captain had reason to insist, also should be met with reward. There was yet a further distraction for his military mind; the sister monarchy to the Bourbon régime was rocking. Revolution threatened the throne of Spain. A French army of invasion was despatched to bring about stability, and old soldiers of the days of Napoleonic wars, such as Captain Barbier, shook their heads at the stupidity, remembering how veterans of Tilsit and Austerlitz had been bogged down in a Spanish war of disastrous attrition. Fear soon fell away. The French invasion was so surprisingly successful it was more of a military procession. Then, with that distraction resolved, came the news that *émigrés* who had lost their land might receive a thousand or two francs, at the most. So, later in the year, the Captain turned his mind again to recognition of *écriture nocturne*, convinced that, by rank and by birth, he should be given some worthwhile recognition. He went, once again, to the Institut du France to enlist aid from the Academy of Sciences to advance his system by demonstration. He told the savants how his method of instruction to the blind had been "rendered to an extreme simplicity which would make it available to poorer parents of blinded children who would be able to instruct themselves". The Captain was confident enough to add that "The results are such that it must raise the morale and improve existence for many unfortunates and make their lives useful to our society."

The Academy responded to this gleam of hope. It selected two reigning stars of science to put the Captain's claims to the test. It organised a visit to the Paris institute by Professors de la Cépéde and the immortalised André Marie Ampère, the "Newton of electrical science", the technical genius whose name now stands for a unit of electric charge shortened to the amp. These two eminent scientists applied empirical test to establish what could be done by reading fingers with the Barbier code. They did this by placing pupils in different rooms to eliminate tricks of memory. When they left the institute, the two scientists were satisfied that there was a future for the columns of raised dots. Ampère, with literary flair for which his son would also become known, declared: "M. Barbier's system of 'night writing' is an art of speaking to the touch."

The report from the two sighted judges, Ampère and Cépéde, gave new respectability to the Captain's code; so much so the Institut du France advanced him an award of a thousand francs (a goodly sum in that day) to continue refinement and popularisation of his invention. But while the money jingled in the Captain's pocket, his stocks with the more deeply involved people had slumped by his insistence that his code was the final answer for the blind.

A whole century later blind Pierre Henri would castigate Barbier for "preconceived and uncompromising opinions", and say that the path to evolution of the original notion of raised dots had been blocked by his "aristocratic prejudgements".

More in tune with the time, the Director of the Paris institute, Dr. Pignier, offended by the Captain's doggedness, wrote:

As with most inventors, Captain Barbier has allowed his mind to become exalted with thoughts of the great advance he has created. Thus his need for self-gratification had become more important than trying to understand the true and real needs of the blind. Regardless of its merits, he has pressed his method onto other people and has exaggerated its merits. He cannot recognise that a method for soldiers to communicate with each other in the dark of night is not necessarily ideal for blind persons . . .

Director and Captain were in opposition. Neither could know that a seed had been planted in the mind of the boy from Coupvray, and that this seed would germinate and bring changes far beyond anything either of the two sighted men could have hoped for.

It did not come in a swift flash of genius. It grew out of the realisation that the blind had to tread the same pathway as sighted people. It was born from persistent dedication to objective, and it faced a long, patient climb to a summit of reasoning so pure it seemed like simplicity. Louis Braille, both as youth and man, shed the flawed philosophy of the past to attain his masterpiece in a style now reckoned to be genius.

There was no special moment, day, week or month, when it could be said that his creation was achieved. In retrospect, it seems that his whole life and its events had been the training for the task that would free blind people from ignorance and indignity.

There had been signposts on his journey to immortality; history touched his childhood and brought blindness. His father compensated with the simple alphabet boards and added high sensitivity to the gift of adept Braille hands. There was early spiritual training and the blessing of people whose interest lifted him to the institute where the stage was set for the realisation of his remarkable gifts. Finally, Captain Barbier's ambitions touched his mind and endowed him with his life's work.

It has been argued that without Captain Barbier's ability and persistence there would have been no Sonography, no raised dots, and thus no Braille. The argument is hypothetical. It is as valid as saying that without the German, Röntgen, the Frenchman, Becquerel, the New Zealander, Rutherford, and his English colleague, Soddy, Albert Einstein would never have expounded the theory of relativity and subsequent explanation of the nature of matter in the cosmos. Without question, Barbier's punched dots offered a means to an end, but that end was reached through high talent and clarity of thought, and was light years beyond mere adaptation. As the man on the spot, Director Pignier, commented, "To change things in the way that Braille did was not innovation, but pure invention."

A century later, blind historian Pierre Henri would declare that Louis Braille did much more than perfect Barbier's system: "He turned it upside down and created it anew, so that even if the blind do not owe the whole system to Braille, they owe to him all that is best in it."

In truth, raised dots for finger-reading gave Louis Braille no more than a starting-point from which to depart, from the traditional approach, to totally original thinking. He did not know, any more than Charles Barbier ever knew, that they were following a path that had been taken by others in the past. Unknown to them was the Egyptian reference to a scholar of the fourteenth century who produced raised heiroglyphic writing; they did not know of the Spaniard, Francisco Lucas, who pre-empted the first steps of Valentin Haüy with letters carved on wood to aid the blind; or of attempts by an Italian scientist, Gironimo Cardano, who had trodden Barbier's road to raised symbols; that in their own city of Paris, two centuries earlier, a Pierre Moreau had pressed metal type into paper to create raised texts; that a German inventor, one Georg Hardsdoeffer, had worked for years trying to produce a code for the blind based on raised geometric shapes. In all that long and fruitless search for the ultimate answer, only Louis Braille, given the base of Barbier's raised dots, attained the summit. And if the code of night-writing-cum-Sonography was the launching pad, it was the brilliant mind of the teenage blind boy from the village of Coupvray that made the soaring journey of original thought to success.

After a dozen years of blindness, and by the fifth anniversary of his admission to the Paris institute, the son of the village saddler was bent on a course that would lift him to greatness. In the first grey

169

weeks of 1824, a year to be climactic for France and for the world's blinded people, he opened a period of intense study with a determination phenomenal for a teenage student. Director Pignier had seen the burgeoning talent in the previous year when Louis Braille had carried off first prizes—for book studies, handcraft and music—and so had promoted him to senior student status in charge of a hand-working class. In the weeks of the opening of the year Dr. Pignier saw a youthful prodigy at work:

When the day's work was done, and when others were resting, I would find him sitting in some quiet corner with the ruled board, paper, and stylus. Sometimes he would fall asleep in utter weariness from constant search for the great benefit he was to bestow on the blind, and thus earn their undying gratitude . . .

The dedication to objective was remarked on by other boys. Promotion for Louis Braille and his companion Gauthier in the musical studies meant a standing with other pupils, and they were listened to with respect. And among younger students was Hippolyte Coltat, who all through his life with Braille at the institute would remember the day when the two Academy scientists, Ampère and Cépéde, examined students on the use they could make of Captain Barbier's writing system. That same night, lying on their straw pallets in the chill dormitory, Gabriel Gauthier had argued with Louis Braille on how the drawbacks in the night-writing code could be eliminated; and Coltat heard both lads decide they would try to develop a better code. Louis Braille had then commented: "The methods we now use take up too much room on the paper, and too much time. We have to think of space! We need the least possible number of signs to express our thoughts."

Hippolyte Coltat would grow up in the shadow of Louis Braille, would become a renowned teacher of the blind himself, and would make the valedictory oration when Braille died. For him, the remark on that winter night typified the concise mind, the clarity of thought that would be shown— in study, in music, in crisis—and which in the outcome would bring a triumph so that Coltat would cry out, in public: "O blindness. Are you such a misfortune when you can inspire such results?"

As with other young pupils of his time, Hippolyte Coltat lived with Louis Braille through the sacrificial burning of energy and mental resource, knowing how, day by day and week by week, Louis Braille did not flag or falter in the drive to find a doorway through which the minds of blind people could break free from their "dark stockade". In retrospect, for Coltat, the engrossment of Louis Braille and its final price were heartrending. A century later, in Paris, near where the old institute had stood, Helen Keller captured the picture in her mind of the young Braille of that time, working through the small hours, experimenting with paper and board and stylus and falling asleep in the midst of his work. "It moves me inexpressibly," the famed lady said. "He was, literally, wearing himself out."

In those early months of creative thought, Louis Braille made no distinction between night and day. Scheduled studies, handcrafts, devotions in the old St-Firmin chapel, walking to mass at St-Nicolas-du-Chardonnet, even his music, were all interruptions in the process of singling out an elemental truth from the faults of the Barbier code and in forming the concept taking shape in his brain. Through freezing winter nights, sitting at daily meals of soup and bread, walking damp corridors, his mind was ever seeking a method through which the blind could come to the shining world beyond those ancient walls, to have access to tales of adventure, travel, fine conversation and great music. At fifteen years of age he knew there could be no emancipation for the sightless without learning through books.

In his clear mind he processed lines of argument into channels of thought that brought him to the first cornerstone of his ultimate solution. His youthful wisdom said, simply, there was a vital difference between "touch" and "feeling" for the fingers of the blind—a distinction that sighted authority had never understood.

He recognised how, when the sighted eye ran left to right along a line of type, the eye did no more than present the brain with an alphabetical arrangement that the cerebral cells could convert in a flash to patterns with meaning, expression, emotion, instantly recognisable. Thus, his first cornerstone was a simple truth: it was the brain that read the words and not the eyes!

In his reasoning it followed that fingers could also present a recognisable picture to the brain, just as swiftly, just as certain as to meaning. There was the critical leap of imagination, the truth that flooded his dark world with shining hope! And there was the essential distinction between "feeling" and "touch".

Feeling was to trace the shape of letters in the old Haüy-style embossed texts; feeling was the traverse of Barbier's columns of dots and finding the cipher to give meaning, in sound, in phonetics. But —touch! Touch was utterly different. To his seeking brain, touch meant resting only fleetingly on a line of raised signs running left to right, and framed down in size to be within the compass of the nerve cells of the fingertips, which could then transmit a picture of *alphabetical* meaning to the brain, just as speedily and efficiently as the eyes. There was the problem. What form of signals, what raised signs could he use to fit the pattern of reading fingers that travelled only from left to right? And further complication faced the progression of his concept. He had to begin experimenting in reverse! To create his raised signs on sheets of paper, which he carried up to the dormitory at night, he had to make the impressions from the *opposite side of the sheet*! Every sign, every word he tried to form, had first to be turned around. He had to work not from left to right, but from right to left.

Through the weeks of blossoming spring, with the resumption of the rope-walks to the Botanical Gardens, and memories of Valentin Haüy and his brother, the Abbé, both of whom had died the previous year, and on into lingering summer, the mind of Louis Braille knew no respite from his chosen mission. So intense was his search that when summer brought the annual prize-giving, his name did not appear among the awards. It was the one blank year in all his time of studentship. Director Pignier noted this, and understood the omission from the close watch he had kept on this unusual youth. When the summer vacation came, he made a point of speaking with Simon-René Braille, when the father came to take his son home on the stage coach to Meaux. The Director never recorded his advice to the saddler, except to remark on the love the father bore the blind lad with a biblical reference, how it was obvious Louis Braille was "the Benjamin of the family".

Dr. Pignier was also impressed with the bearing of the village saddler, and saw him as a man of probity, whose manner and habits were "reminders of men of the *ancien régime*, respected and esteemed by all who came into contact with him". The mutual respect born in that summer meeting would be shown later, at a time of grief and struggle.

In the August homecoming of 1824, Simon-René and Monique Braille saw in their son a metamorphosis of the deprived child they had nurtured through the bad years. He was changed, taller, and more solemn; the airedale curls were still tight and fair on his head, but his face was drawn, the skin tight over his cheekbones, and he smiled rarely, even in the joy of reunion. The cottage was soon quiet again. Both his sisters were now married with homes of their own; and so also was his older brother, Louis-Simon, but he came several days a week to work as an assistant to his father. The first days saw the renewal of acquaintance with old family friends and with cousins from nearby villages; his father took him walking to the vineyard to feel the warmth of the sun on his face, and to hold the fattening bunches of grapes in the palm of one hand; he made solo journeys up the steeply cobbled La Touarte to sit near the old school, where one day there would stand a statue in the square that bore his name. And he would go often to pray in the cool of the grey stone church. But, always, he was preoccupied with the thoughts surging through his mind.

As August advanced, the drive within his being led to lonely days of contemplation. He would have sheets of rough paper in his hand and go to his father's workshop, to the bench where he had been blinded by his own hand all those years before, and he would take an awl from his father's line of tools—a "sharp pointed instrument"—and leave the cottage. Running his hand along the curving stone wall into the laneway of the Chemin des Buttes, treading through clumps of buttercups and nettles, he would climb to where the giant chestnut threw its shade across the grass, and there, with the mighty trunk at his back and the sounds of birdsong and the hum of insects in his ears, he would hold the paper on his knees and make patterns of dots with his father's awl. Day after day he would be in the same spot, and the sight of his slim figure bent over the paper became commonplace.

The mind-picture of Louis Braille, in the dank gloom of the ex-seminary, working on his system into the winter nights, had been "inexpressively moving" to the brave Helen Keller: had she been able to envision the intense youth in his home village, seated under the huge chestnut, a thin figure in his institute uniform of drab blue twill, the line of brass buttons shining in sunlight he could not see, she would surely have found the scene heart-warming. For this was the time of great achievement. What he did on those summer days of solitude would change the future for blind people in many lands.

There was nobody then who understood the grandeur of his task. Week after week, villagers passing by would see the blind lad beneath the tree and nod their heads knowingly; and some would meet with Monique when shopping in the Rue St-Denis, and smirk: "Saw your Louis again today, Madame Braille, still sitting on the hill playing with his pinpricks."

People of that era never knew how the days of "playing with pinpricks" saw the workings of genius. Indeed, the world would never know how, or when, in that summer the talent of Louis Braille broke through to the code that would resist all challenges and remain supreme. Nobody now knows from whence came *the star of genius that lit the world of the blind*.

The author of those words, M. Serge Guillemet (sightless Director of the modern Paris institute for the young blind), has suggested the Braille system can be understood by touching each shoulder and each hip in turn to represent the first four dots of the Braille pattern, and then add two more points for each knee. This clever illustration moves the mind to the picture of the devout blind lad searching for the pattern that would meet his needs, and to see him at prayer in the grey-green church on the hill in Coupvray making the sign of the cross, four points of obeisance that could be rearranged in his mind to form a small square to fit within the compass of the nerve cells in his fingertips, four raised dots, which, in variation, could give him ten separate signs, all running left to right for the reading touch.

Could it have happened that way? It is speculation, but an explanation many will find acceptable in the light of the spirituality that marked the life of Louis Braille. It is supposition, as is the suggestion of how he might have gone on, from the four-point square, to his final pattern of six dots, the so-called Braille "cell". Time and again, in many parts of the earth, the product of the blind lad's inspiration has been connected with the simple game of dominoes. Constantly, the Braille "cell", the frame of dots used to indicate language in a hundred different tongues and thousand dialects today, is likened to the "domino six". Legend in that corner of the soft rolling Brie country where the Braille "cell" was born suggests a strong link with the game of dominoes. That summer, when the blind lad worked on the form of his code, the game had moved into France from its country of origin, Italy, and was popular in the bars and taverns of Paris. It was avidly played each day in village *auberges* in Coupvray, and in Chessy, where Braille's cousins lived.

Could a set of the twenty-eight little boards have come under the fingers of Louis Braille? Would that have suggested to his mind that within the compass of six points he could represent the whole alphabet? Louis Braille was ever modest, always loath to speak of himself, and he neither confided nor wrote of how that "star of genius" came to his mind. He left no clue. Yet the link is close enough to conjecture whether the similarity between his final fingertip pattern and the "domino six" was more than coincidental.

The weeks of the summer of 1824 could not bring instant perfection. No matter how intense his concentration, agile his fingers and sensitive his touch, he could not at once attain the ideal code. But sitting beneath a tree on a hill in the village of Coupvray, picking away with his father's awl at sheets of rag paper, what he did achieve was the beginning of an immense advance for blinded people. Refinements would come later, but he was at first base. His six-point "cell" would fit within the compass of normal fingertips; his first four points could be extended with variation of a bottom couplet to give more than the basic letters of the Roman alphabet. There was enough diversity in his "domino six" pattern to consider provision beyond the normal letters.

His six dots were numbered as points. Starting with the left-hand side of his frame, the top dot became Point One; that beneath it Point Two, and in the bottom left-hand corner was Point Three; on the right-hand side the dots from the top down were points Four, Five and Six. Point One represented the Roman letter A; Point Two added to that first dot gave the letter B. Thus by the variation of his top four dots he could show the first ten letters of the alphabet. The next ten letters, from K to T, were indicated by adding Point Three, the dot in the bottom left-hand corner. Addition of the sixth dot, Point Six, to all the previous signs gave him a further ten signs, which completed his 25-letter alphabet (he would include the rarely used W in later refinements) and allowed five accented vowels. Then he used his basic four-dot square signs with the addition of the bottom right-hand dot (Point Six) as symbols for all the accents —grave, acute, circumflex and so on— commonly used in European languages.

He then made two further additions to fill the void left by Captain Barbier's system. A specific prefix to signs from the top four dots converted them to numerals; thus, with the special prefix the letter A became Number One; and so his signs ran from One to Zero—all the numbers that would ever be needed. Now he met the crucial need in language which night writing had ignored: punctuation! The same beautifully simple device was used. Another specific symbol converted his numerals, or his first ten letters of the alphabet, to commas, colons, full stop, plus brackets, and to marks for quotations, questions and exclamations.

Louis Braille had sat alone in long session through that summer vacation working with his father's awl on sheets of paper. It was Hippolyte Coltat who would observe that in any comparison between the achievement of Captain Barbier and the fifteen-year-old youth it should be remembered that Louis Braille had only his fingers and his brain to guide him, yet he had devised the answer to the age-old problem afflicting people without sight. But it would not stop there! The intellectual leap of the summer of 1824 was the beginning of a life's work and a monumental contribution to easing deprivation and suffering of fellow human beings. Said Coltat: "He never lost sight of this work. Never for an instant did he shirk the task of refining, developing, and practising his new way of writing and reading."

Hippolyte Coltat had a retentive memory, and in those crucial times in the Paris institute he absorbed details of character and style as Louis Braille grew from adolescence to manhood. He noted how, despite clarity of mind, brevity of speech, and a searching and direct honesty, there was an amiable disposition and kindliness that cloaked sheer modesty. And Coltat would say—and Gauthier agree—that the natural reserve in Louis Braille's nature held him back from trumpeting his triumph to the world at large. They were the first people to whom Louis Braille confided that the blind now had, for the first time, an alphabet of their own. They were the authorities of their day, but others would follow those two young blind men: experts, such as Dr. Richard Slayton French, former head of the California School for the Blind, who said of the Braille code: "Like the Roman alphabet itself, like Morse code and other greatly simple inventions, it bears the stamp of supreme genius."

During the last days of that summer vacation of 1824, Louis Braille heard the bell in the tower over the old grey church toll a doleful message. The nation was in mourning. King Louis XVIII had succumbed to the years and breathed his last. Apprehension was widespread, since the royal departure was reckoned to be the end of ten years of recovery after the tribulations of the Napoleonic era. Back in the heady days of April 1814, when Bonaparte had first abdicated, the King's younger brother, then the Comte d'Artois, and appointed Lieutenant-General of France for the occasion, rode into Paris two weeks before Louis XVIII returned from exile in England. Greeted on that happy April day by cheering crowds and decorated streets, and led to Notre-Dame where a Te Deum was sung for him, the Comte d'Artois found his belief in the divine right of the Bourbons firmly cemented. He was never to shed that eighteenth-century conviction —to his sorrow. He became Charles X, and was crowned in Reims, where Kings of France had been anointed for some 1300 years, but he presided with foolish use of power over a nation still with the theme of equality, liberty, fraternity running in its mind. History would rate the new monarch as addlebrained and staggering from blunder to blunder as though pursued by perverse fate. Had he set out to ensure that there would never be another Bourbon on the throne of France he could not have been more successful.

His brief reign would prove for the inmates of the old ex-seminary along Rue St-Victor, as it did for the nation, a disaster.

The world's first institute for the education and care of blind children, founded by Valentin Haüy, no longer had the shield of royal interest. The near-simpleton new monarch had little interest in trivia such as ninety blind boys and girls living on state charity in a derelict building. Their lot was left in the hands of politicians and uncaring bureaucrats, none of whom had either inclination or imagination to waste on the invention of a fifteen-year-old village boy.

Among the pupils under the guidance of Director Dr. Pignier, none the less, there was high enthusiasm. No tag, such as Sonography, was tacked onto the new code. The reading fingers of pupils and blind tutors perused the system, among them Hippolyte Coltat, who recorded that the Braille code met requirements from the start. He wrote how its beautiful simplicity, "put it within the grasp of anyone willing to give a week or two to learn the symbols". And, in that flush of appreciation, Coltat declared:

It allows blind people to record secret thoughts, to put on paper their impressions and feelings, to express ineffable longings and emotions hitherto known only to God. If we blind people were not held back by the characteristic modesty of the author of this system, then we would proclaim him the Jean Gutenberg of the blind!

Gabriel Gauthier, of the musical talent, was more practical. It was apparent to him, as it was to Louis Braille, that improvement and precision in the placing of dots in writing the code was essential to its wider use. They agreed to work together so touch could be applied with accuracy. In the woodwork class they shaped a board about the size of the normal school slate, and cut parallel lines of triple grooves, crossways. They fitted a frame to this on which a brass grille could slide up and down, and in this grille were open faces through which the dots of the "domino six" pattern could be accurately imprinted. With this device a blind person could set the paper under the sliding grille and, working always in reverse, from right to left, could find the exact spot on which to make the raised point on the opposite side of the page. The work on the board was finished early in 1825. It was the first Braille *planchette*, the first step towards technology that would become everyday routine in future for people without sight.

With Dr. Pignier's approval, many more such *planchettes*—or writing boards—were fabricated for pupils to learn the new system. The Director recognised quickly how the hope he had held out for the work of the Captain of Artillery had been realised by the blind youth. Dr. Pignier later would write:

The value of Braille's new code rapidly became apparent, and its advantages were quickly noticed in the work of the students. For the first time, pupils could take notes in class in the same way as sighted people. The enthusiasm was such that some children set to work to compile their own Braille libraries and works of reference by making extracts from textual works and putting them together in volumes. It must be admitted that writing by means of raised dots gave study at the institute a boost.

The effect on speed alone was remarkable. Dr. Pignier cited how one senior blind student who took lessons at the Sorbonne had astonished his professor by how quickly he could take notes in Braille, and read them back without faltering.

However, the downward turn of national events, loss of confidence in the new King, and the obstinacy of officials worked against adoption of the new writing code for the blind. Braille's mentor and supporter, Dr. Pignier, gave discreet encouragement, but in the committee of governors, in ministerial echelons and ranks of civil servants in the Department of the Interior, there was still a solid bastion of indifference. Change was opposed, because it was change. There was yet another threat implied in the Director's recommendations: money was involved as much as new thinking.

The coterie of Count Alexis had spent years dragging necessary funds from the grudging bureaucratic purse-holders, even with the help of the late King's fading interest, and they feared the wrangle that would ensue if it proposed the whole bank of teaching materials at the charity institution should be thrown away and replaced with new volumes, with raised dots, of all things! This invention meant not only a whole compendium of new books, but a new method of printing!

And there were other cogent reasons: the loss of positions was feared by sighted teachers, who could anticipate blind persons taking over their role. They argued it was vital that watching briefs should be held over sightless students; and this could be done without everyone learning the new code of "punch-writing". Behind all the objections, however, was the entrenched attitude that what was good enough for sighted people was good enough for the blind. They, too, should manage with the normal Roman alphabet. This outlook was so powerful it was natural for authorities to shake their heads at the notion of spending money on a new-fangled scheme of raised dots.

Economic conditions were also used to

deny the introduction of the Braille code. Severe depression was spreading across France. In the ten years of restoration under Louis XVIII the population of the country had grown by upward of two million, but there had been little compensating increase in productivity from either farms or factories. Napoleon's imperial adventures had bled the nation of the cream of young manhood, so that initiative and entrepreneural activity was at its nadir. Unemployment was rife, with one man in two out of work in many regions, making great numbers dependent on state charity. Gloomy forecasts abounded and made it easier for officials not only to deny innovation, but also to cut back levels of support that had been routine in the time of the old King.

The first bite of austerity came on the blind inmates of the ex-seminary in the early months of 1825. Savage cuts ushered in two years of restriction and near-penury, during which time the affairs of the institute were brought close to collapse. Days and nights were cold with a reduction of fuel supplies; the daily diet was forced back to subsistence levels akin to those before Dr. Pignier's administration. The Director was moved to anxiety by what was happening to the inmates; and knowing his voice would raise little concern in the departmental corridors, he called again on friends in the Faculty of Medicine to intercede, and this time Professors Cayol and Récaimer brought with them a consultant with the high-sounding title of Doctor to the Children of France.

When the bureaucrats of the Ministry for the Interior went home for Christmas 1825, they had just read a terse report on the conditions at the Royal Institute for Blind Juveniles. The doctors' statement was succinct; it did not bother this time with the state of the building. They concerned themselves with pure survival! "Given the poor state of health of these children and the work they have to perform, they must be given an improved diet. They must have more food, and, what is more, food of better quality."

The brevity, the portent implied, caused little concern and, sadly, roused no action. As the new year moved into deep winter, blind pupils and tutors still tapped their way through crooked corridors to the refectory for their daily sustenance of bread and soup heavily laced with gelatin to give a filling effect. They still drank untreated water drawn from the Seine; they still lived in conditions and putrid emanations that took a toll of health and energy. All too often Dr. Pignier filled his role as doctor; again and again he had to confine sick children to the ill-lit dank infirmary for special care; and it was noticed how occasionally there would be a visit by a priest to administer last rites, and a bed would remain vacant in the dormitory. Normally empty places would be quickly filled from among thousands of blind youngsters throughout France. Not so from the first months of 1826. Then the screws tightened further. The Government forbade increase in funding to meet rising costs; a terse ministerial decision slashed by one-third the number of places that would be financed. The institute archives paint the dark picture that ensued:

The result was disastrous. No more blind children could be accepted. Studies got behind or lapsed with staff shortages, it was no longer possible to replace tutors and students capable of conducting classes or to supervise workshops, because they would have had to be kept on beyond their time. The reductions also affected the teaching of music. The institute's orchestra, which had been productive, and of which all were proud, would have been destroyed if the austerity went on for too long. The whole establishment was threatened with disintegration.

There was a further blow. A bookkeeper, appointed to keep watch over the financial affairs of the institution, managing its Government income and its earnings, absconded with a sum equal to one half of the annual budget. In these dire circumstances Dr. Pignier struggled through with the aid of donations and an anonymous legacy. A subsequent report was to comment that "the institution was in a deplorable state".

Hard times, lack of official interest, poor diet and the general depression could not curb enthusiasm for the new Braille code among blind students. Out of view of sighted teachers, in the night when oil-lamps were out, fingers worked on mastering the system of the "domino six" pattern of raised dots. In the dark the blind pupils and tutors practised the speedier, more suitable method of writing and reading. Knowing this, Dr. Pignier was discreet, and continued to obey the dictum of authority: the old embossed books were still used in the classrooms.

Louis Braille had reason to be exultant, but he was not satisfied that the ultimate had been reached; nor would he ever be content to rest as long as he lived. There were refinements, amendments, contractions to be devised to reduce still further the space needed, such as being able to use both sides of paper sheets and to increase speed of reading and writing. At the same time, he had to complete his education, and this he did with his usual flair and style, again figuring prominently in the annual awards. But this was to be his last year as a student. In the decree of Louis XVIII, which had lifted the blind juveniles from the squalor of the Quinze-Vingt hospice in 1815, there was a limitation of a maximum period of eight years that an inmate might spend at the institution as a student. Thus, late in 1826, Dr. Pignier faced losing his gifted protégé by the royal edict. Before the advent of Louis Braille's eighteenth birthday, however, the Director found the solution in a later amendment to the decree, which allowed him to appoint the best students to a small, élite band of junior tutors, despite the burdens that had fallen on the institute.

Louis Braille was assigned to conduct classes in geography, grammar, history and arithmetic, to supervise the slipper-making workshop and give piano lessons, all for the return of board and lodging plus two francs a week.

Apart from status, the promotion brought few other privileges. As it had been with Dr. Guillé's *répétiteurs*, these tutors ate at the same table of the same food, slept in the same dormitory, were subject to the same disciplines, and had to pass all private correspondence, inward and outward, through the hands of a sighted teacher or the Director. They could have occasional visitors, however, and were allowed to walk out on Sunday, though not to miss meals or mass. Outings could be made with one of the young sighted pupils, and for Braille it was a treat to tread streets he had first walked with his father, hearing the noises of the life of Paris, smelling cooking in basements, recognising fragrances of types of meals his mother had cooked—so long ago it seemed.

In these difficult years Dr. Pignier saw his reward in the young man's growing ability as a teacher. Though not yet twenty, he showed remarkable balance of control and authority. In an era when the rod and threat of isolation in dark cupboards were routine, Braille used only persuasion and example. Coltat wrote of this ability:

He conducted his lessons with deep understanding of the special problems of the blind and he taught with such charm, mingled with sagacity, that the students hung on his words, and his classes became such a pleasure that they not only held him in esteem but also saw him as a wise and trusted friend.

The effect of Braille's amiable disposition

and quietly reasoned manner went beyond the classrooms. Students and seniors and tutors would ask him to arbitrate in some dispute or argument and, Coltat remembered, he would resign himself to the task, saying, "Well, someone has to sacrifice themselves for peace." Because of this readiness to settle differences he earned the title of "The Censor". Yet, for all this, his closest friends found him too retiring, unassertive, with a lack of awareness of his own importance; and that rankled, because his talent and his wonderful code had been given no recognition beyond the student body.

Gauthier was particularly irritated by this. "You are too modest, Louis! We know here what you have done, what you try to do, but those people out there know nothing and will care nothing unless you tell them. Speak up and demand the honour due to you!"

But the inclination to be unobtrusive, to be humble, was too ingrained into Louis Braille's nature, and his friend's criticism could not arouse change—or cause offence. His personality drew great strength from his faith: "I believe in the

Father Almighty, maker of heaven and earth and all things visible and invisible . . ." He was part of the Catholic Church, and the credo gave him the philosophy to soften hard fate, so that he could speak to his students of the *"fortune of going blind"* so early in life. "The older you are when blindness comes, the harder it is to adjust. Being able to adapt when growing up makes being without sight more a handicap than affliction. The spirit is not crushed as heavily as being sightless in later years. That is why knowledge is so important to us younger people. We do not want to be shut away from the world because we cannot see and so we must work and study to be equal with others, not to be despised as ignorant or objects of pity. I will do all in my power to help you all attain dignity through knowledge."

The essence of his message to his blind students was a gift of himself, a selfless, total dedication of his power of thought and of his time and energy to their cause. Through the time of austerity he worked at daily lessons without complaint, still using the old embossed books, knowing that his students would benefit greatly if his own code had been fully utilised. But there could be no official introduction of the "domino six" code. The message from authority made that clear, and was final. But official frowns, cuts in staffing and student numbers could not smother the surreptitious use of the Braille six-point "cell". Now there was a more certain, speedier pathway to the treasury of prose and poetry, wonderful beyond dreams. Yet, for Louis Braille the tutor, it was but the beginning. He was never seen as a fighter, a battler for rights, but behind the serene sightless face and the quiet manner was spiritual strength.

The fertile mind from which had grown the beautiful simplicity of the code of six dots could not rest on laurels, even among fellow inmates. He would never be proud enough to be content with what he had achieved. There was improvement always to be won, and he sought perfection. To be all-embracing, the code would need amendments, symbolic signs, contractions that moved writing and reading towards stenography, abbreviations for quicker use of the method. And all this mental seeking took place in the quiet hours when the long day's duties were over, week after week, on into spring and summer, until the institute was again facing another year of shortage and the rising toll on health.

The new winter loomed over Paris, and Dr. Pignier's anxiety mounted. Early in December 1828, he turned once more, in desperation, to consultants at the Paris Faculty of Medicine. They came in a phalanx, this time, specialists and consultants, including as before Professors Cayol and Récaimer, and the Doctor to the Children of France, Professor Baron—and others. And this time they railed against "an outrage" that had kept youngsters in these parlous and perilous conditions for far too long. Their report was a condemnation of inaction and indifference. Afflicted young people had been left in surroundings that had not only taken toll of health but had claimed a rising number of lives. The doctors reaffirmed the disgraceful condition of the ancient edifice, first deplored seven years before: floors wet and cold, covered courtyard and so-called gardens muddy and wet; poorly aired, low-lying, too near the river, and subject to those dangerous "putrid emanations". They declared:

> The shortcomings of this place are serious. They will not diminish. The ill-effects persist, and in the years since the first report the health and well-being of both inmates and staff have been severely compromised—despite the care taken. In this last year, especially, there have been a prodigious number of illnesses from which several children have died! This loss of life must be attributed to the conditions in which they live. We are certain that the institute can no longer be safely housed in these premises with such dangers to the health and the lives of all the inmates. The establishment should be moved to large, well-aired, more salubrious surroundings.

The effect on authority of that report was long in coming; another ten gruelling years would pass before the matter would become a public scandal, long over-ripe for correction. But, whether it was coincident or resultant, in the next year there was some easing of restrictions on student numbers; an increase of twelve youngsters was allowed, taking the total to 72; but Louis Braille and his contemporaries continued to work, to exist and strive for betterment, in conditions the Faculty consultants had rightly pronounced as "perilous to life".

A second—equally vital—contribution to the emancipation of the world's blind people grew out of Louis Braille's "domino six" code. Although a consummation of his fingertip pattern of six dots, it was by itself a pinnacle of creative thought, of pure reasoning sprung from intellectual yearning. He was just twenty years old, in his seventeenth year of blindness and his tenth year as an inmate of the Paris institute, when he unlocked the door to the world of written music for the reading fingers of the sightless.

As with his original code of raised dots there was no swift flight of imagination to produce an equally beautiful simplified system of musical notation. Rather it came from the same kind of gestation, months of mental search and sifting, and the same simplification of complexity to reach what has been widely acclaimed as the stuff of genius. In keeping with his natural modesty, Louis Braille left posterity no account of the hour, day or month when he reached the solution to the problem of placing written music under the reading fingers. All that is known for certain is that in the midst of austerity, subsistence diet, cold days and night—and no official recognition—he worked to satisfy the hunger in his soul, the hunger in the hearts of all blind music-lovers, to have access to the rich sources of written works.

The world will never know what mental agony was suffered by the young blind man to reach the outcome; in devoted pursuit of his objective he wasted not a word on his own emotions nor told of his sacrifices. We can only imagine the long solitude of the struggle that led to final triumph; to see him in the mind's eye, in the hours when he was not engaged in tutoring, bent over some keyboard—thin, pale, undernourished, fair curls awry— utterly immersed in the sounds his touch produced; to vision him at the organ in an old church giving expression to music branded into memory by sheer repetition, the newly appreciated Bach Mass, the St. John Passion, the heart-moving "Agnus Dei" ("O Lamb of God who taketh away our sins . . . Maker of Heaven and Earth and all things visible and invisible . . ."), to understand his longing to reach out for other jewels of composition from what the poet Longfellow would term "the universal language of mankind".

Music was a window through which Louis Braille could reach the unseen world of tonal brilliance, sheen, beauty of movement. The hunger for musical riches had grown from the day he first touched the raised scores in Valentin Haüy's book of plain chant and simple tunes. Music, mingled with spirituality bred in boyhood, pulsed through his mind to give him a serenity that later would be likened to "angelhood" and called "Christ-like" by Helen Keller. And this yearning for deeper and more expansive expression was heightened by teachers from the Conservatorium with knowledge of the development of liturgical music in France, from the original Gregorian chants to the great sixteenth century composer Palestrina, and all the riches that flowed from them. It would have risen as a wonderful challenge for him to open a door on the treasury of sound.

It is known that Louis Braille began to structure his musical endowment on the old institute piano. Music was still a teaching subject, and as he had given the blind their own alphabet to gain access to literature, it was natural he would turn his mind to breaking down barriers to written music. Hippolyte Coltat left a record of this time.

He was gifted with great patience during this attempt. His methodical mind broke down and analysed the problems, and he gradually made imperceptible, but real, advances, tackling at first plain chant, then simple melodies, and then, on the piano, working on more complicated scores.

Blind historian Pierre Henri sees Braille's progress also as a step-by-step advance, and says: ". . . nothing was more simple than the way he gave values to musical expression. He started from a new principle with the tonic sol-fa scale and the piano keyboard."

Louis Braille knew of other attempts to illustrate musical scores in relief, of complexity and convolution built into methods of showing the notes of music by numbers and raised letters. He held out for clarity and, importantly, for a method that would fit the touch of a fingertip. He had provided for the written word with his alphabet signified by raised dots; now he realised that he could use the same system to illustrate written music.

Eight of the first ten letters, indicated by the top four dots, served as the tonic sol-fa scale and he was able to choose, from the many remaining arrangements of raised dots, symbols to indicate such things as change of octave, keys, tempo, expression, and the various forms of notes. With judicious selection of raised prefixes Louis Braille covered the whole range of musical composition—a result never before achieved.

For the first time blind musicians could not only read written music but could also compose their own music, using the same simple Braille *planchette* with its triple grooves, remembering always that the music they composed had to be written in reverse, to be read by touch. The brilliantly simple concept would, with few modifications, prove an endowment beyond price for uncounted legions of sightless music-lovers.

While in the confines of the Institut Royale des Jeunes Aveugles the six-dot Braille code was unchallenged as a method of communication, the outside world continued to disregard the invention. Authority, in the form of the governing committee and the Ministry of the Interior, stubbornly insisted on previous teaching methods, clinging to the old dictum that "the blind must always be brought closer to the seeing". Raised type was still the prescribed method of tuition, but the "domino six" code was used in quiet defiance by the blind tutors and sightless students. Notes were taken openly by use of the Braille board and the "stiletto" and, almost every day, tests and experiments were employed to increase skill and speed. Braille himself is said to have punch-written extracts read by a sighted teacher from the English poet John

Milton's writings and to have read them back without hesitation. To this was added out-of-hours work to increase the facility built into a pattern of dots that fitted the fingertips.

Word of the enthusiasm was bound to spread. It came in time to the ears of the originator of the raised-dot code of "night writing", Captain Charles Barbier, who was still working on his system, utterly convinced that his was the great leap forward and Braille a mere adaptation. His reactions indicated a resentful jealousy, and his subsequent writing displayed the condescension of a superior to an upstart youngster. In the year of the creation of the six-dot code, Charles Barbier had lain claim to his system as being "the basis of education of the blind".

Five years later he complained to Dr. Pignier how his *écriture nocturne* system had been deformed, and still claimed his system to be "the fundamental basis for teaching of the blind". He justified the grant from the Academy of Sciences with printed publications of his work; yet, while his friends in the Academy and among the coterie of Count Alexis de

Noailles nodded their heads in sympathy, the blind juveniles and the tutors continued the process of proving the true value of the six-dot code.

Captain Barbier's vexed attitude, however, finally broke down the wall of modesty in Louis Braille. He was persuaded to place the basis of his superior code on record. The skill had been established within the institute to do this, facilitated by the benign attitude of Director Pignier. The boys had transcribed extracts from standard works of French grammar into compendiums of Braille, and some metal types had been cast so that sheets of Braille printing could be impressed by hand. All this was in preparation for the issue of Louis Braille's first publication. And so Louis Braille announced the milestone he had reached in the cause of the blind. The Director regarded this landmark publication as so important that he no longer averted his official eyes, but at request handwrote the words Louis Braille dictated for this first publication, the text of which would be peppered with examples of the Braille code.

It was a small volume, some thirty-two

pages with a long title! *Method of writing language, plain chant, and music, by means of raised points for the use of Blind Persons*: "Author, Louis Braille, tutor, Royal Institute for Blind Juveniles, Paris". This historic document, giving the blind their own alphabet and access to music, was concise, in typical Braille style, an explicit and detailed exposition of the new system, with illustration of the grooved board and what was called a "stiletto" for achieving the raised-dot patterns. The book was printed in embossed text, which made it readable by the fingers of the educated blind, but also visible to the eye. For the international effect that would follow, it was an unpretentious production; and, though at first it seemed to be stillborn, it would in hindsight be reckoned the true public manifestation of the Braille code. It made no immediate impact on sighted authorities, and a further five years of refinement would pass before the thirty-two pages were to be exhibited, along with works actually printed in Braille, at the annual summer Industry Fair held in the Place de la Concorde.

There was some excuse for official disregard. The years were marked by insurrection, abdication and revolution. Blood was spilled again on the cobbles of Paris; workers were slain by royal troops in the silk-weaving city of Lyon. In Paris some two thousand rioters and soldiers died amid wanton destruction, pillaging and burning. Surrounded by civil strife in which mobs broke up funeral rites, sacked a church along the nearby Faubourg St-Germain, and burned the great library and the archbishop's palace at Notre-Dame, inmates of the old seminary building on Rue St-Victor stayed behind the thick mouldy walls. There were no outings, no rope-walks in the Botanical Gardens. The Director grew increasingly anxious as troubles developed into the July Revolution of 1830, when Charles X fled Paris by coach to Bordeaux and set sail for safe exile in England. What the fate of the institute and these blind juveniles would be nobody could then guess.

There had been two spectral figures as responsible ministers in less than two years. Deputy Martignac, whom the King had put at the head of his chosen gaggle of ministers, had been too busy fighting for survival even to know of his charges in the institution, and just as transient had been his successor, Deputy la Bourdonnaye, whose name had, ominously, been linked with the so-called White Terror that was marked by acts of vengeance in the early days of the restoration. Then he, too, was gone, along with the last of the Bourbons, and in place on the throne was the former revolutionary soldier, the Duke of Orleans, whose father had been guillotined in the Place de Révolution, who yet would take his title as Louis-Philippe, King of the French.

In the upheaval there was little relief for the pupils, tutors and staff of the institute for the blind. The number of students was increased by one dozen as a concession, but there was no extra funding to provide the improved quality and quantity of food the eminent doctors had requested as long before as December 1828. Soup and bread remained the staple diet, and the blind young continued to live in dangerously unhealthy conditions. Yet their determination was undaunted; they continued to work and study, trusting the future would bring them reward; and it was in that atmosphere and setting that the use of the six-dot code became a daily practice.

Late in May 1831 the Director unexpectedly summoned Louis Braille to his quarters. There he heard the voice of his brother, Louis-Simon, solemn in greeting, telling him with tears while holding his hand that Simon-René Braille had died. Their father had lived to age sixty-seven, had served his family by working at the old wooden bench where Louis's adventure with one of his tools in infancy had ended in blindness. He had died where Louis's life had begun, in the bedded recess off the room where they had all eaten together across the years. And Louis-Simon, in his grieving manner, told how Simon-René's last thoughts had been of the welfare of the "Benjamin of the family", the son who was loved above the others.

The blinded young man, now twenty-two years old, was left with a deep and abiding sadness. His father was gone, begetter of his life, whose face had vanished early in his nineteen years of blindness, on whose shoulders he had ridden as a young boy! But there were memories more recent, his father's strong artisan hands, kindly voice, the smell of leather, even in Sunday clothes, walking the cobbled hill to devotions together in the old church, strolling in the vineyard to feel grapes that would make the family wine.

Nothing seemed to ease the pain of loss. Hippolyte Coltat saw his grief as "tender and beyond the limits of duty". His father had been a warm presence, with the character the sympathetic Dr. Pignier would paint for him: "A man who was a reminder of former days, esteemed and respected, an honest saddler—a man of probity . . ."

And because the respect was mutual, Simon-René Braille, in his last hours of life and with deep concern for the future of his blinded son, sent his plea with Louis-Simon to Dr. Pignier: "Please, please—never abandon my son. Never, never."

The Director had dozens of young sightless people for whom he was responsible, for their well-being, education and training for life, but this young man, distinguished by singular ability, integrity of mind and

216

outstanding qualities as instructor of others, held special claim. The dying plea of the village saddler imposed no unwanted burden. The obligation was accepted gladly, and many years later Dr. Pignier would attest that he had accepted the obligation imposed by the father's last wish as a "sacred legacy". He filled the gap in Louis Braille's life with consolation, counselling, encouragement; and his caring was so evident that he would later be accused by detractors of showing favouritism. The rapport was strong.

The following summer, when his brother escorted him back to Coupvray, Louis Braille used his special skills to earn money to aid his widowed mother. He travelled the Meaux district tuning pianos, and in this time received a letter from Dr. Pignier urging him to be heartened in his task. He wrote back, in pencil, his free-hand forming wavering letters, to say how grateful he was that the Director, with all his work, was thinking of him while he was away from the institute. He wrote of grand balls and dances held by the rich people at local châteaux and how he had been tuning their pianos:

Sometimes I have to stay the night in one of these fine houses, and the experience seems illusory after living in the old seminary. But I have tuned a number of pianos, and had I been even more enterprising I could have ended up pretty rich. For the time being, I shall remain in Coupvray, enjoying the country and the air and getting myself ready to recommence my classes and studies at the end of the month with even more zeal than before . . .

There was warmth and affection in the letter, and the closure of the letter was as though he was writing to his father. That same tone would be found in all their future correspondence: a future that would be marred by shocks, separation and sadness, but which never would lessen the bond between them. Dr. Pignier upheld his "sacred trust" beyond the requirements of duty; and in supporting Louis Braille in the coming years of strain and trial made his contribution to the emancipation of the world's blind in the role of surrogate father.

An epoch opened for the sightless people

of the world in the decade of the 1830s. By this time centres for educating and training blind persons had been founded in many countries, and international attention was naturally fastened on the pioneer establishment Valentin Haüy had brought in existence some sixty years earlier. Other historic events marked the beginning of an era that would liberate blind people from age-old shackles of ignorance. With King Charles, the last of the Bourbon dynasty, in exile, Louis-Philippe, the first Orleanist king on the throne, there was in France a flood of creative culture, art, literature, drama, poetry, to distract attention from a gradual change of attitude towards the blind juveniles and tutors in the old Paris building.

Through the first years of this decade a stream of visitors began appearing at the Institut Royale des Jeunes Aveugles, eminent social workers from other countries, people involved in their efforts to care for the blind, notables from Belgium and Germany and Austria, from England and Scotland, and from the United States of America. There was the illustrious Austrian humanist Johann

Wilhelm Klein, who had founded his own version of the Haüy institute in Vienna, but had balked at the Braille code, arguing the blind had to use the same alphabet as sighted people. There were pioneer workers from Liverpool and Edinburgh; and there was the redoubtable American fighter for freedom, black-bearded Dr. Samuel Gridley Howe, the so-called "Lafayette of Boston", who was so impressed by the Paris methods that he recruited one of Dr. Pignier's teachers to go back with him to Boston's famed Perkins School for the Blind, where he would educate Laura Bridgman, the first blind-mute to be taught to read and write, and who would later communicate with Charles Dickens (in person) and be forerunner to such people as the inimitable Helen Keller.

The effect on the lives of the inmates of the Paris institution, as these visitors came and departed, was to be lasting. Gradually, light dawned in official minds that in the heart of Paris was a humane innovation of national prestige. Here was the first such institution of its kind in the civilised world! France had led the way in this example of humanity to unfortunate human beings. Pride could be taken in inventive talent and innovation that was NOT allied to military adventure and conquest! Yet eminent foreigners still had to study this in a decaying edifice. They walked dark, crooked corridors, trod worm-eaten staircases, sniffed the acrid tang of mildew, and inhaled those "foul emanations" of which doctors had complained and warned a dozen years before. Even so, with economic restraint still to be argued, change was grindingly slow, extra money grudgingly allotted. However, by 1833, Director Pignier, true to his vow of 1821, never to cease the struggle to better the lot of his blind charges, won a classic victory. His senior students were appointed as the first fully fledged teachers of the blind. From then on the blind were able to teach the blind; and the outcome of this decision would stretch on into the future to where, a century and a half later, a blind man, M. Serge Guillemet, would direct the modern institute, a situation that could never have been envisaged in 1830s, even with such gifted people as Louis Braille, Gabriel

Gauthier and Coltat on hand and equipped to serve their fellows with dedication and understanding.

Dr. Pignier was funded to form this élite corps of blind teachers, among them Louis Braille, aged twenty-four, and Gauthier, aged twenty-five, and to pay them 300 francs each a year plus board, lodging and clothing. He also added symbols of status to their drab, dark-blue brass-buttoned uniforms, badges of academic palm-leaves made from gold thread sewn on the lapels; and though these ornaments of authority could not be seen by their owners, they were a distinction worn with pride both inside and outside the old building. Later these blind teachers would be allowed the honoured title of Professor. From this time, Louis Braille blossomed as a teacher of unusual ability and effect, in written and oral language and in musical study. Many future teachers were his students. He trained men as organists who would hold their places in famous churches throughout France (and one of his pupils was the blind son of Sir George Hayter, who was then principal artist to the royal house of Windsor in England). In his records, Dr. Pignier described Louis Braille's teaching skills as "precise, clear, his explanations to the point. Without unnecessary elaborations, he was always willing to reiterate his teachings if his students had not at first properly understood."

The years brought other pleasing recognition of his talents; his alphabet for the blind was shown at the exhibition in the Place de la Concorde, with actual productions in Braille—the pupils had themselves impressed condensations of popular school books on French grammar —and he had the first gracious acknowledgement from the originator of the use of raised dots, the ageing Captain of Artillery:

I learn with interest the method of writing you have composed *for the use of persons deprived of sight* [author's italics]. I cannot praise too highly the generosity that inspires you to work for those who share your infirmity. It is wonderful what you have achieved at your age; it says much of the feelings that guide you.

Charles Barbier wrote his comment in longhand script and sent it to Dr. Pignier to read to the young blind man; it had the added comment that the Captain would have written the words direct had he had enough time to master the Braille code. At the same time, however, Charles Barbier was preparing a further small edition on his *écriture nocturne* system, and he left this comment in the foreword,

. . . it was M. Louis Braille, a young student and latterly tutor at the Paris institute for the blind, who first had the idea to reduce the writing of raised dots to three lines, making my system easier to read with less space. He has made other applications of the method which recommend its use in an establishment concerned with teaching blind children. We are grateful for this important contribution.

It was never in the nature of Louis Braille to downgrade other human beings or to decry their efforts; he showed his own quality of grace in the second edition of his booklet, when he wrote:

It was M. Charles Barbier who first thought of representing sounds and articulation from a series of raised dots in various combinations. This was ingenious and he allowed me to modify his method to produce a new way of writing for use by blind people.

As the blind historian Pierre Henri would observe, it would have added to the lasting credit of Captain Barbier had he "learned to be a good loser". But to the end, through years of Louis Braille's astonishing adaptations—of musical notation and the first mechanical means of writing in the code of the "domino six" pattern—Charles Barbier held stubbornly to the claim that it was his system that was aiding sightless people to reach out to new horizons; even though, in that same year of Braille's first exhibition, the young blind man was awarded another tribute to his talents, the accolade of permanent organist at the historic church of St-Nicolas-des-Champs, where he would perform some of the first musical works ever translated into the Braille code.

With this appointment a new heart's

warmth came into the life of Louis Braille. For the next five years, on Sundays or when special masses were held to mark some religious festival, he would leave the dank building on Rue St-Victor for the church of the holy vision. With a young sighted pupil at his side as guide—and guardian—he would walk the crowded streets of old Paris, head high, face serious in concentrated thought of the music he would perform. Proud in his blue uniform, with the gold palm-leaves bright on his lapel, they would cross the river near Notre-Dame, the air acrid with the tang of charred wood from the ruins of the arch-bishop's palace—a testimony, in his mind, to mob madness—and they would tread the length of Rue St-Martin to the stone pile that was the ancient church of St-Nicolas-des-Champs.

As the music he culled from the vener-able organ washed over his consciousness, Louis Braille could draw strength from the legends stamped into memory and learn lessons from the lives of great people of the past, of the power of faith, which gave the strength and resolution that would equip him to fight the impending personal trial.

Before he reached his twenty-seventh birthday Louis Braille knew his years were numbered. He knew the mark was on him. The first signs came in physical weakness, faltering steps on the old wooden stairways, walking to and from the church, breathlessness, giddiness, weariness from work. It had happened to others before him in this place. The seeds of death were in his lungs, heritage of the "foul emanations". There was, however, no indication in Louis Braille of a sense of final ending. It was as though strengthened spirituality brought a tempering of hope, as well as the compassion of charity. He went on his way, more intent than ever on the objective that had become the mission of his existence: the perfection of a simple, effective means of communication for the blind.

5

The Last Radiance

BLOOD first stained his pillow in the late winter of 1835. He was just twenty-six years old and the (then undescribed) germs of tuberculosis were feeding on the tissues of his lungs. He had previously been seized by bouts of coughing and had pushed the portent of terminal consumption into the back of his mind, but once the blood spilled on the pillow he could never again start coughing without fear of haemorrhage that might end his life. From now on friends and family saw a change of manner; the bright smile came less often and he became more intensely preoccupied with his work to help make the blind self-sufficient. Dr. Pignier watched him, noting how, "from the start of this illness he had sombre forebodings. His letters showed evidence of dark thoughts that came into his mind and

228

This sketch of the historic building is all that remains of the St. Firmin Seminary where Saint Vincent de Paul worked and prayed and which later became the home of the world's first school for blind children.

The ancient church of St. Nicholas du Chardonnet, on the faubourg St. Germain, where Saint Vincent de Paul once worshipped and Louis Braille was confirmed and later played the organ.

Eloquence and compassion, voiced for the first time in the French National Assembly by Deputy Alphonse de Lamartine – poet and humanist – won not only a new home for the blind children of France but also hope of dignity in useful occupation.

The 13th century church at Coupvray where Louis Braille was baptized when only four days old. The tower has since been added but the original baptismal font is still in place.

Braille's birthplace, the cottage in Chemin des Buttes in Coupvray now maintained as a museum by the World Council for the Blind.

Tools of the trade, now mounted behind glass on the wall above the bench where the child infant was blinded; centre the *serpette* and to the right the bradawl, either of which could have caused the historical injury in the workroom of what is now Coupvray's Braille Museum.

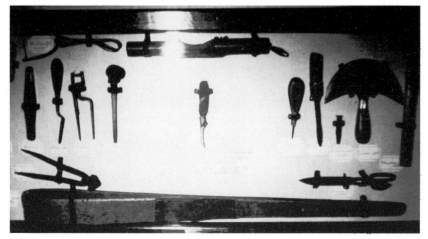

Known after his death in 1822 as Apostle to the Blind,
M. Valentin's compassion for a sightless beggar-boy
led to founding the world's first school for blind
children, the school in which Louis Braille's genius
flowered.

sometimes the same premonitions would slip into his conversation."

His former student (and now teaching colleague) Hippolyte Coltat saw no sign of fear in Louis Braille at this ominous time. He wrote:

His firm and lively faith gave him nobility of sentiment and helped him to face the approach of death without fear, if not without emotion. He took the wise precautions of regular habits and extreme sobriety, and this seemed to improve his health so much that he sometimes entertained pleasant prospects for the future.

The sixteen years Louis Braille had spent as boy and man in the antique building had laid their claim. From then on, all he undertook to do, all effort he gave to his life's work, the kindness, love and compassion he showed to his companions and his blind pupils came from strength of commitment to his objective. There were periods, in the nature of the illness, when he was offered the illusion that his body was overcoming the colonies of bacilli penetrating his lungs, and though he took brief hope from this manifestation, Coltat would observe: "his profound intelligence and rectitude of mind allowed him to foresee the chain of events and their consequences".

As Louis Braille felt death brush his cheek, as his slight body grew steadily weaker and his step began to falter, so the activity of his mind was sharpened into urgency. Time became a precious commodity and weakness a challenge. There was still so much to do to complete his life's mission. Around him were the world's only experts in the use of the "domino six" system. Outside the institute, in the minds of decision-makers and holders of national purse-strings, there was opposition to what he knew in his heart, and intellect, was the true path for the blind to follow to break free from those "age-old chains of darkness" that bound them to ignorance and uselessness. Sadly, sighted officialdom was blind to the advantages of the six-dot code and stood rockfast on the view that inmates of the institute should be kept to the Roman alphabet. Their attitude was close to that of the unlamented Dr. Guillié, who, twenty years before, had declared: "The blind are not like other people . . . not liable to be restrained by external demonstration . . . and can only judge things by extremes."

Those who could not see could not know what was best for them! They needed to be instructed and to do what they were told! It was continuation of the ancient outlook: the blind were not like other people, and so there could be no yearning in the minds of these sightless juveniles to reach out and touch the cultural treasures of civilisation. What good to them were storehouses of literature, knowledge, science, music? They would have to make do with simple embossed books and learn a manual trade —weaving, basket-making, to tune pianos —or play the organ in some parish church.

The sighted opponents of Braille would yield no ground; not even in the face of evidence that the persistent inmates provided of their faith and belief in the six-dot code, when in 1837 they produced the first full-length book in Braille. This was an astounding effort. Students and blind teachers worked as Trojans in their spare time for two years. With niggardly resources and their own pitifully few francs they toiled and sacrificed so that hundreds of pages could be produced and bound into volumes using the very alphabet discouraged by authority, by the Count and his coterie, by bureaucrats up to Minister of the Interior, Adolphe Thiers, former journalist, publisher and then rising star in the Government under Louis-Philippe. (Louis Braille had written to this politician of his new code and its advantages, and had not been given the courtesy of a reply.)

Not all the opposition to Braille by sighted officials was outside the institute. Director Pignier gave what help he could to the use of Braille among the pupils, he provided tools and materials and other equipment so that each student could have his own *planchette* and stylus, as any normal child would have pencils and writing pad, but he put himself at risk by going against the official policy. His support of Braille was to be used for his undoing. His chief teacher, assistant to the Director, M. P.-A. Dufau, was rigidly opposed to the use of a different alphabet for the blind. He gave no help to Louis Braille's undertaking, but stored facts and details away in his mind for when it was opportune to move against his superior.

Dufau was ambitious and cunning enough to hold fast to the official line. He would argue, once it was safe to do so, that "use of this code of dots can only turn the blind further back into their own closed world". He would not argue this openly until by intrigue and betrayal he had attained his own ends. And so, he stood like Iago, silent in the shadows as the big book was produced, watching a continuing labour of love that would have battered its message into more sensitive minds.

It was all done by hand, by touch, in hours outside the normal day-long schedules of classes, handcrafts, devotions, meals. It finally appeared in 1837, an astonishing testimony to the value of a code that authority denied. It is not known who chose the work to be transcribed, but it was a popular school manual of the times; written, it is believed, by two Jesuit priests, Fathers Philippe and Anaclet and, titled *A Summary of French History*,

Century by Century, it had a synopsis for each royal reign. The transcription hand-pressing was carried out by blind teachers and students; large pages of good quality rag paper were used, thick and stiff enough to provide firm, raised patterns of dots; punches and presses were fashioned, each page held twenty-seven horizontal lines with each line having upward of thirty symbols. Since this took up much more space than letterpress printing, the whole work was divided into three separate volumes, each containing some 200 pages glued back to back, for the first time in a Braille document. The finished work weighed some 4 pounds, or almost 2 kilograms.

This book was historic. It was a rebuff to opponents of the "domino six" system of communication. It did not ring bells in bureaucratic minds, however, but instead generated animosity against the man in charge of the establishment, who had patently encouraged, if not deliberately assisted, in an act of defiance of official policy. Also remembered in Ministry corridors was the nagging campaign that had been conducted by Dr. Pignier since his appointment in 1821 to provide new accommodation for the few dozen blind pupils, and in which he had enlisted leading doctors and churchmen. The time, though, was not yet ripe for either the Count, or the bureaucrats, or the ambitious man in the institute who coveted the top job to exact penalty.

The first decade of the Orleanist rule under Louis-Philippe saw a change in public attitudes. The late Napoleon Bonaparte had been restored to a place of honour, his effigy placed on the column in the Vendôme—albeit in civil dress—and plans were afoot to ship his coffin back from St. Helena's rocky slopes for interment among national heroes in the Invalides. There was also a second renaissance, with explosions of art, literature, drama, opera, music, along with claims for freedom of speech and the liberty of man, all freshly burgeoning. Sharing the prospect of a brighter future, in spring 1838 the Institut Royale des Jeunes Aveugles, in Rue St-Victor, was approaching a first shining summer of hope.

May 14. Couples were strolling again in the woods of Champ de Mars and the shady paths of the Champs-Elysées. With winter gone, trees along the Seine were draping a green curtain. In the heart of Paris, high above the National Assembly, flags were fluttering for a meeting of Deputies—flags no longer white with the *fleur-de-lis*, emblem of the rejected Bourbons, but the red-white-blue of the tricolour of the revolution, flags symbolic of change, dramatic change, in the character and attitude of men who thronged the national arena. Powerful and eloquent orators, men imbued with ideas on the spirit and dignity of man generated from years of rebellion, could give voice to argument and opinions that could have cost them their heads, or life imprisonment, in previous decades. Although this was still a time when calls for financial restraint echoed through the Chamber, there were many who sought redress for past neglect and indifference. On this special day for the chosen blind children of France, the new Minister of the Interior, Montalivet, produced a bill that in cost, if not intent, aroused controversy.

The Minister was seeking a budget allotment of the munificent sum of 1,600,000 francs to house some hundred boys and girls. These were blind children, however, and among the Deputies support was strong. Dr. Pignier had prepared the ground for this day. The magazine *La Moniteur universel* had been in print to support the views of the panels of doctors, charging, "There has been great mortality among the young blind people! Their lives have been compromised by the disgraceful and unhealthy conditions in which these select children have been incarcerated . . ."

Now the battle was to be fought on the national stage. The hour had come for the first public denunciation of the indifference that had inflicted suffering and mortal disease on helpless children. Two Deputies had armed themselves by a visit to the decaying ex-seminary in which Louis Braille and his fellow unfortunates had suffered for more than twenty years. There was Deputy Meilheurat, and with him famed poet and humanist Alphonse de Lamartine, a passionate defender of human rights. It would not be generally known to the majority of the blind people of today how the poet's eloquence played an important role in the epoch about to open. A born aristocrat, noble in mind, manner and purpose, on this day Lamartine stood with eyes blazing in the National Assembly, and with an impassioned speech denounced the indifference that characterised the nation's attitude to its sightless citizens.

Alphonse Lamartine himself had known indignity, humiliation and fear. Educated by the Jesuits, he had seen his father flung into a revolutionary prison by the vengeful *sans culottes*; he had fled for safety to Switzerland from the hated Corsican Usurper; he had come back to serve in the bodyguard of Louis XVIII, had met and speedily married Maria Ann Burch, said to be connected by marriage to the Churchill family. He had campaigned for the rights of workers and the poor, had been elected Deputy in 1833, and was in the high tide of a remarkable career. This day his oratory was aimed at redressing the lack of concern of the nation for the blind, and to castigate the tolerance of filth and disease in the institute, which he had been to see for himself. He told his fellow Deputies:

No words of mine can give you a true picture of this narrow, putrid, dim place, of corridors cut in half to make veritable boxes which they dare to call workshops, or classrooms—of twisted, decrepit staircases—Oh, so many of them—worm-eaten and rotten! All of this, far from assisting these unfortunate children, who can only feel their way, seems like a challenge thrown down before them in their blindness. There are some who would return these children to the Quinze-Vingt, but I shall fight that tooth and nail! To put this school for blind children into a home for aged invalids would be utterly cruel and dangerous! So, I simply say that never will budget money be better spent than in restoring dignity and morality to those from whom nature has stripped one of their most precious senses! If this whole Assembly was to rise now and go *en masse* to this place, the vote for this bill would be unanimous. And if tight-minded economists chide you for making this money available, then, let me say—the blessings of hundreds of children restored to a life of intelligence and useful work will absolve you.

The Director of the Paris institute was also absolved. Dr. Pignier had won his long struggle. His charges were to be set free from cruel years of groping their way along mouldy walls in a maze of corridors! Lamartine's appeal carried the day, Montalivet's bill was passed by the Deputies, clearing the way for the choice of a more convenient site for an entirely new building. This was to be on the famed Boulevard des Invalides, at the corner with Rue de Sèvres, the street in which the Lazarite chapel had been located. On that corner, flanked by what is now Rue Maurice de la Sizeranne, a million or more francs would be spent to create a magnificent new home, into which Dr. Pignier had long dreamed of one day leading his sightless students and teachers. But that dream would never be realised.

The scheming Dufau, conspiring with his cabal in the Ministry, would usurp Dr. Pignier's place and impose his own stamp upon the legacy of the late Valentin Haüy. Before that could happen, however, the inmates of the Paris institution had to survive a further five long years in the old residence of St. Vincent de Paul.

As his illness progressed, Louis Braille found the call of Coupvray increasingly appealing. In long days of pain and sickness in the dreary old seminary he could find some comfort in memories of home, the ease, the love, the soft fragrance of the Brie country, sun on his face, sitting with his mother, talking with his brother and sisters, eating the rich cheese and drinking fine wine from the family vineyard. So it was easy to persuade him that he could recapture health and vigour in that simple sanctuary. And at one time he caught the illusion of recovery from weeks in the fresh air and strolling near the Marne. It came about from the kindness of his surrogate father. Dr. Pignier, always watchful, became concerned at the young man's appearance, and sent him home to spend a month with his mother, to breathe "the air that would cleanse the lungs". At the end of that time Louis Braille wrote his benefactor: "I shall be back with you next Monday. You will not find in me a

Samson, but you will see a man, thin, but not skinny, enjoying reasonably good health—thanks to your kind solicitude . . ."

In truth, he found only temporary relief from the stamina-sapping infection, and no release from the mind-driving mission that waited at the institute, duty to his pupils, his music, his friendships, and the compelling work of seeking what he now called "social rapport" for people who could not see. Affection, respect and anxiety among his companions led them to urge him to live in the Brie village. But he resisted. When Hippolyte Coltat sought to persuade him that he would regain full health in the quiet village life, Braille told him, with typical realism: "There is no need to dissemble with me, my friend. You know I don't use that kind of false currency."

Duty held him fast to long days with endless hours of conceptual thinking, ceaseless experiments and displays of what his friend would describe as the "force of character and will power". Dismissing fear and refusing to give way, he displayed calm acceptance of the burdens of fate. Neither did he resent the hostility that people such as Dufau and the remote officials showed towards his new method of writing. Instead he saw this lack of understanding as a gulf to be crossed by more efficient communication.

"Those with sight," he argued, "will not take the time or have the patience for the few weeks' study required to master this code. They will not come to us—so we must try to go to them. We must discover a method of writing that *both* blind and sighted people can read. We must communicate."

He discussed his aspiration with the Director, who noted the ambition in Louis Braille was as much from the heart as from the intellect, and wrote of this new attack on sightlessness:

For this young teacher it was not enough to have invented the system of reading and writing that would deservedly earn the eternal gratitude of blind people. He wanted his blind fellows to have more contact with sighted people outside the walls of the institute, to be able to correspond, and so become more self-sufficient.

243

In this daunting task there would be many false trails, copious hours of working with brain and fingers, seeking and finding disappointment, always with illness sapping his reserves and his resolve. The facts reveal the agony of mind behind months of searching for the solution he craved. Dr. Pignier's words tell what he observed in his last years as Director.

We had long used some guiding devices for handwriting, with pen and pencil, and he had written his own letters in this way, but this never satisfied him, because the method did not bridge the gap both ways, between sighted and blind. He had the co-operation of another fine blind student, a M. Binet, and together they experimented with a method of printing letters, with small plates we had cast for the purpose, which were pressed down by hand on blank sheets of paper under coloured tracing paper, so that with the two sheets they had both impressions and the printed characters. He knew of other attempts to form letters with dots, which had not been satisfactory, and he believed he could find a better system.

Louis Braille, not yet thirty years old, his vitality sapped by four years of insidiously progressive illness, and still confined to the dank ex-seminary, was bound on another undertaking with mind and fingers, mental and physical powers stretched to the limit in his struggle to break still farther from what Coltat had called the "shackles of blindness". There survives a word-picture of the ailing young teacher that describes him as "slender, of medium height, head bent slightly forward, fair hair awry, commonly serious of aspect, but with his fine features sometimes breaking into the bright smile of his youth . . . an elegant man whose originality consisted of not appearing to be original".

Louis Braille's dedication was also apparent. While his days were crowded with normal teaching schedules and musical instruction—and some of his pupils would later take up posts as organist in famous French cathedrals—he could still find energies to assail the new citadel he had planned to reach. Dr. Pignier wrote of this period:

> With the patience of genius, persistence and consistency, he reached his objective. The calculations and experiments with combinations of dots and signs were countless, until he finally framed his method of displaying with raised dots the figurative letters of the alphabet, punctuation, and numbers.

This first step to build a bridge between blind and sighted persons was nowhere near as simple a process as Pignier described. To enable the blind to correspond with sighted people, without resort to the scrawl of pencil or pen, Louis Braille had to create a new concept. Nothing existed on which he could improvise. Being blind, he understood, says blind historian Pierre Henri, that to read the correct shape of a letter of the alphabet it was better to create a numbered board giving the horizontal and vertical co-ordinations of each raised point rather than the simple shape of a raised model. Methodical as ever, Braille framed his new code (later given the name of Raphi-graphy) with the many calculations and combinations of which Dr. Pignier wrote.

Yet more was needed than this. His friend, Hippolyte Coltat, wrote of this need as "a fine regulator to guide fingers to correct spacing and siting". And this was a need that would be solved by yet another of the legacies from the devoted life of Valentin Haüy. Some thirty-two years before, when the Founder had fled from the *sans culottes*, he had taken one of his brightest students with him to work in Germany and Russia. That student, Alexandre (Remi) Fournier, now aged forty-eight, came back to the institute where he had been educated to offer his technical expertise to Louis Braille in fabricating the "fine regulator" needed to guide hands of the sight-impaired. Remi Fournier had spent his adult years at the Quinze-Vingt hospice teaching manual skills to aged blind inmates and was on the verge of retirement to Versailles, where he planned to educate his own, sighted children.

Working together in the workshop at the institute, the two blind men finally fabricated a frame and sliding grille that gave precision to the use of a punctuating stylus in the hands of blind writers. Louis Braille composed yet another pamphlet to explain the code of the dotted letters and their application, but it was still too slow. Years later, the opponent of the original Braille code, Dufau, would write of this regulator as "an ingenious creation, one of those curious works which should never be overlooked in historical analysis". Like others of his time, Dufau could not see how this "curious work" not only would lead to adaptation and improvement in the hands of future students of the institute, but also would open a gate to far more astonishing developments.

Braille's booklet on Raphigraphy was written in the usual concise style. One of the longest sentences was its title: *New Method of Representing by means of Raised Points the shape of letters of the Alphabet, Geographic Maps, Geometric Symbols, and Musical Notation—for use of the Blind*. With the name of the author already distinguished among the sightless community, the work drew attention and a demand for supply of the regulating grille and grooved frame, so that when Louis Braille came back to Paris from his summer vacation in the autumn of 1839, the most adept handcraft workers at the institute were already employed on production of the equipment for Raphigraphy, which Dr. Pignier was selling for around fifteen francs each, enabling him to pay welcome pocket-money to his young workers. The demand was bound to be short-lived, from the limitations in the nature of the system, and as Louis Braille faced the trials of the coming winter months with the feeling that his major work was finished, there came yet another temptation to leave the old building, a chance to live in clean air a life of comparative ease.

The offer would have been tremendously hard to resist. Louis Braille, in the last decade of his life, was suffering increasing debility, with the attendant depression that his illness imposed. He still groped his way through the old St-Firmin Seminary building; each winter month his mind longed for the peace and quiet of Coupvray, while his weakness drew him closer to the time when he would have to shed daily teaching. In these circumstances the letter from the Austrian benefactor Johann Wilhelm Klein would have strained every thread of his loyalty and resolution.

Klein was still opposed to the use of the six-dot code. He held the same view as Dufau, that it would shut the blind away from the rest of the world. Just the same, such was Louis Braille's reputation as a teacher, he was offered the post of personal tutor to a single blind boy, none other than a prince of the royal blood of the Hapsburgs. There was temptation! To live in royal comfort, be well paid, eat the best food, give gentle instruction to another blind person, and, most of all, breathe the clean, healing air of Alpine heights. Yet, even this magnetic appeal could not break the hold on Louis Braille's mind and heart. He could not turn his back on his pupils, and—most powerful reason of all—there was still work to be done in pursuit of his life's mission. He wrote to the sighted Austrian, using his new Raphigraphy, politely declining, and adding: "For the unfortunate one, whose fate I share, I have the honour to offer this new small method of writing. I am your respectful and humble servant, L. Braille."

There was yet a further sacrifice to be made during that winter. It came to his ears how one of his best musical pupils, who had recently left the institute, had fallen on hard times and, with a mother to support in rooms in Paris, was in need of help. Louis Braille's act was to surrender his post as organist at the historic church of St-Nicolas-des-Champs on condition the appointment be offered to the poor student. Coltat said this was typical of Braille.

There were many examples such as this of his generosity and kindness. Friendship was to him a tender feeling, as well as a duty, and he would often sacrifice time, health and money to befriend some person. It was one of the attributes that has given him a place among those who have worked hardest to break the chains of blindness.

Friendship was a bond so powerful it turned aside the offer of a useful, yet easy, life with good food, status and prospects of a renewal of health and verve. Fidelity in Louis Braille imposed a lasting companionship, which was tightened by sharing a mortal legacy from years spent in the rotting environment of the Paris institute. He was not alone in his illness. Similar seeds of tissue destruction were at work in the lungs of his dearest friend. Gabriel Gauthier would become his companion in death, as in life. Both men knew their fate by 1840. Both understood that there was no cure for consumption, so only a miracle could intervene; and both found comfort and joy in music, and in sharing that joy with each other. Denied certainty of life, just as both had been bereft of sight in childhood, their minds and aspirations plumbed deeper waters than those reached by normally sighted people. The loss of a faculty had delivered a broader version of enlightenment. Blindness and looming death had opened a door to hitherto untapped reserves of will-power and dedication. In these times, people who knew Braille would remark on the depth of emotion and tenderness in his organ playing. Dr. Pignier recorded how

Braille's musicianship earned flattering comments for "lively and brilliant playing". Hippolyte Coltat wrote of Braille's style at the organ as "brilliant, clear, precise, as was his personal character". Breadth of interpretation tenderness for the rich field of liturgical music he could now reach, also appealed to senior priests of the Lazarite order, and that would shortly bring him great comfort and solace.

Gabriel Gauthier also made remarkable progress as master-teacher of the organ, cello, piano, and as a composer of serious music. A year older than Braille, he had been born in a Loire village, in the Department of Saöne, and with the same rural background as his friend always enjoyed the thought of summer weeks in the open air. Later he would find it tiring to travel to his home, and he spent some of his time with Braille at Coupvray. By then he had completed his master works, including five volumes of *Répertoire des Maîtres de Chapelle*, his song series and cantatas, all exquisitely punched in Braille notation. Also, Gauthier had filled with distinction the coveted post of organist at the historic church of St-Etienne-du-Mont. Thus the lives of the two men were linked. It followed that with their common love of music, their similar background and shared characteristics of creative nature, they were both subject to the hurt of unexpected loss, vulnerable to the event that struck their lives with brutal suddenness in early 1840.

The dismissal of Dr. Pignier was as swift as it was cruelly unjust. One day he was there, and their days under his care and guidance were as they had been for almost twenty years, all their adult lives. Then he was gone, summarily sacked. The scheming Dufau was installed in Pignier's place. The long years of campaigning for better premises, damaging reports of medical panels, the condoning of the use of the "domino six" code in classroom work, and the symbolic rebuke in the first Braille book—the three volumes on French history—had brought retribution from the Ministry cabal. Dr. Pignier was sent packing, denounced for "the unauthorised teaching of history in the school for the blind". Dufau had done his work of character assassination well, persuading officials with his cry of anguish: "The affairs of the Institute are in a terrible state".

The cry was heard by authority, for along with Dr. Pignier the Count Alexis de Noailles, and his coterie were swept away, abruptly, after a quarter of a century of service. Dufau was appointed Director-Administrator. With a new Control Commission, he was armed with a 50 per cent increase in budget, up from 60,000 francs a year to 90,000, and empowered to restructure schedules and standards of tuition that allowed him to shun the use of the Braille code.

The impact of the Dufau coup on the blind teachers and older students was savage. A father figure had been plucked from their closeted lives. In future years when Braille and Gauthier wrote to Dr. Pignier, they would always sign themselves "Your grateful children". They had never envisaged that the man who had fought and won the battle for their new home would be swept from their ken in the hour of his triumph, that they would not hear his step, his voice, or know his guiding hand again. The loss impoverished their lives. Looking back on this bureaucratic act of vengeance from a century on, Helen Keller, with the grief of the loss of her beloved "Teacher" still fresh in mind, would comment that the sorrow that befell Braille and Gauthier and others would have been "more cruel than their blindness had ever been".

The new Director-Administrator of the institute installed himself in the first-floor-room that the great Vincent de Paul had occupied during his years in the old home of the Collège des Bons-Enfants. From there he began an authoritative dominance of a domain he had acquired through stealth and intrigue, satisfied he had toppled his former superior, Dr. Pignier, and that the way to expansion and change lay before him. Dufau continued to oppose the use of the Braille code, oblivious to what a future French writer (Henri Gauvrit) called "the irresistible force of genius, the power of a class of impaired human beings determined to possess life and to mingle with the mainstream of society".

Dufau humbled Dr. Pignier, but he never would defeat blind pupils armed with the inherent strength of the system of the "domino six". They and his own close friend would in time force him to retract and steer a totally different course.

In the archives of the Institut Royale des Jeunes Aveugles the name of Pierre Foucault figures prominently in later association with that of Louis Braille. This is so despite continued tactical denigration practised by Director-Administrator Dufau against benefits emerging from the regime of Dr. Pignier, and also because, as it would be with Braille, inventive genius would not stay bottled up for long by administrative suppression.

Foucault, although a former student at the institution, was not of the Pignier era, but belonged to the time of the shocking merger with the Quinze-Vingt and the later discipline of the formerly dismissed director, Dr. Guillié. He had already shown an aptitude for mechanical invention when he left the institute the year before Louis Braille had been enrolled. Foucault had also been blinded at an early age, from infection when he was six, and his talent would be acclaimed as "prodigious", with some futile speculation on what he might have achieved had he kept his sight. Yet what he did, in collaboration with Louis Braille, was enough for his name to be honoured in the world of the blind.

Foucault was a friend of Remi Fournier, and he knew of the development of Raphigraphy. He, too, had known the need to be able to correspond with sighted readers, and how the system of punching a series of dots in permutated patterns to illustrate letters was far too slow to be accepted for long; it was much slower than the normal Braille code.

The inventor presented himself early in 1841 at the institute and offered to collaborate with Louis Braille. It was a meeting of minds; both men were resourceful, imaginative but realistic, and devoted to "social rapport" for their fellows. Foucault told Louis Braille of his desire to work for improvement and stressed how important it was that blind people should be able "to express their own inner thoughts on paper so their communications would be private and not through the agency of some sighted authority".

Braille's reply was recorded by Foucault:

> Access to communication in the widest sense is access to knowledge, and that is vitally important for us if we are not to go on being despised or patronised by condescending sighted people. We do not need pity, nor do we need to be reminded we are vulnerable! We must be treated as equals—and communication is the way this can be brought about.

Foucault's answer was practical, and speedy. He invented a device he called his Piston Board. The sheer ingenuity of what would be termed the "first typewriter for the blind" seems astonishing coming from a sightless technician. Yet such were Foucault's horizons, afterwards revealed, that it was not at all surprising. The blind man was apparently a frontier thinker in the field of traction mobility. Dufau himself wrote, seven years later:

Who could believe that at a time when nobody had foreseen the immense discovery of new lines of traction—which must change the world—that a poor blind man, knowing only how steam could be used to activate mechanical power, would conceive of what he called his "sliding rail", which, powered by an engine or motor, could achieve travel at speeds then not obtained. This is quite true! Once he had elaborated on his idea, it was made known to many people, who vouch for his inspiration.

But if Foucault's dream of the sliding rail pre-empted the circulating tracks of modern earthmoving machines, of bulldozers and tractors (or Hitler's Panzers) it was still-born for lack of resource or support. Not so the results that in collaboration with the ailing Louis Braille he brought to bear on improving the condition of the world's blind people.

His Piston Board was but the beginning. This ingenious apparatus had ten upright keys, which activated perforators onto rag paper, and the carbon sheet, along the depth of a normal line of writing. These keys could be operated simply by being pressed down with the right hand, while the left hand pushed a handle to align the punches to form the shapes of letters and words through the arrangement of dots. Foucault claimed—and quickly proved the fact—that given a few days to learn the combinations of Braille's new code, normal blind persons could write every word they knew of the French language. With this device, the sightless user could not only correspond with sighted readers and blind alike, the writing itself would always be regular, easy to read.

There was one drawback, which bore on the poor among the blind. It cost some 35 francs to construct, at least double the cost of the simpler Braille-Fournier device. The poor among the blind were compelled to stay with the cheaper apparatus; but the Piston Board none the less had wide usage. In the second half of the nineteenth century it was commonly owned by blind people throughout France and in other countries and later, in 1874, was employed to print a Braille transcription from the French translation of a biography of Benjamin Franklin. The ingenious device won the award of the platinum medal of the French Society for Industrial Development, a triumph that would be repeated for the Braille–Foucault collaboration. But next time the medal would be gold.

The success of the Piston Board fanned a spark in Louis Braille's mind, which flared to inspiration and action. Hippolyte Coltat said:

Until then nobody had dreamed that it might be possible for a blind man to write down the music of the sighted. It had seemed a problem beyond solution. Louis Braille had made it possible for the blind to carry on correspondence with people who could see and read. He decided to try to do the same for music. Again he used his own methods. He started from the principle that aimed at writing that could be set out by a sighted copyist trained in a few basic conventional steps. He then began building improved machines, each one better than the last. To the great satisfaction of his musical friends, he achieved better results than he had hoped for at the beginning of these experiments.

His final amended apparatus could set out the clefs, the stave, the lines above and below, and the notation as well as the words accompanying the music. The system was touched with the same beautiful gift of simplicity that had marked the original six-dot code; the writing of words and music was perfectly legible for both sighted and blind people. Coltat enthused:

A method by which blind composers could make their work known to sighted musicians! This is one of the wonderful legacies Louis Braille left to the great family of the blind. This is one of his titles to glory!

Life under the regime of the new Administrator-Director changed swiftly, disturbingly different from that of Dr. Pignier. Dufau exerted his authority immediately, in many ways arbitrarily. His rule could not be questioned. He was armed with the power of previous experience as deputy head, and this carried weight with the inexperienced Control Commission and his contacts in the Ministry. They allowed him to begin building an enlarged empire, seeing him as a man of words, deeds and vision. The increased budget meant that more staff and more students could be crammed into the old seminary edifice in readiness for the great day.

Dufau's first step was to impose his authority by wiping away much of the past. He began with a swift reorganisation of teaching schedules, which split the student structure in two. He proclaimed: "This institute will no longer be run under the old monastic discipline. Things will be changed so that we can move with the times."

Dufau was a man of words. The education given at the institute, however, would be aimed at self-sufficiency in the outside world. The institute would begin a new era of tuition, with a curriculum to meet the needs of people whose eyes would never see a written word. Pupils would be selected according to manual and mental capacity and be trained either in the primary section to enter the work force in some trade, or be given a higher level of instruction in a secondary section of the institute. But there were limits to classical instruction. There would be little teaching of history, for example, since, he alleged, "Pignier had used history to corrupt the minds of the young blind!" And Latin and geometry would also be deleted. He declared openly: "Go out there, among the beggars, and you will find those who were taught Latin and geometry. Our children are diminished quite enough. We will not coerce them into such things."

Fortunately Dufau did not link the institute orchestra and musical tuition with the days of Dr. Pignier, and so that activity was untouched, which was just as well for the ailing Louis Braille. Thirteen long months dragged by before the first stone was laid on the site for the new home, and in that time his waning strength laid new burdens on his resolution. There was no revival of vitality, no hope of a return to his former verve.

His debility became noticeable. His days were increasingly tiring, with obligatory teaching and musical instruction. His spare hours were spent on improving the

Piston Board device to make it suitable for speedier writing of musical notation. He rarely left the old building these days; he had only the obligation to meet with a gathering of Lazarite priests who had co-opted him to a group of volunteers to work among the poor and handicapped. Even so, when he walked the streets, he still held the shoulder of a young sighted guide, halting every now and again to rest and catch his breath. Seeing this deterioration, Braille's friends, Coltat and Gauthier, suggested a month or so in the country would help him to recapture his strength. Dufau agreed, but said the time would be taken without pay.

Louis Braille was happy to go home to Coupvray to rest and recuperate, and during the first weeks it seemed that with the love and care of his mother, brother and sisters a renewed strength flowed through his frail body. His roots were in this place, and that was comforting. Yet as he began to move about the streets, he knew he was a stranger, an odd figure in his blue uniform with the brass buttons—he never owned any other clothes these days—and, because he wore the gold-thread palm-leaves on his lapel, villagers, accustomed to people in sabots and rough-cut serge, greeted him with the deference they would show to the Abbé or the Marquis. He felt separated from them.

Once again his mortal sickness brought treacherous deception. The quiet and rest lifted strain from his mind, his spirits rose, and his thoughts turned incessantly to the mission still waiting in the dank rooms and corridors of the building on Rue St-Victor. That was an irresistible magnet. While he could still walk, and breathe, and think, the urge was to be back at work among his "fellow unfortunates", trying to improve Foucault's Piston Board, to further his ambition of putting written music under the fingertips of the blind.

On his return to the institute in September 1842 he found change imposed through drastic action. Dufau had acted swiftly and decisively: he had made rapid study of methods for education of the blind being practised in other European countries, in England and America, and had concluded that innovative Paris lagged behind the times. For example, a London doctor named Fry had won a competition staged by the Society of Arts in Edinburgh with a new raised-type mode, and there was a selection of types of raised letters and symbols with such names as Moon, Benowski, Lucas, Alston, Gall and others. He had made a concession to the need for a system that fitted the fingertip, but still remained firm on the use of letters of the Roman alphabet.

A small, raised letter was chosen for the new material to be used in Paris, printers were engaged to produce Dufau's selection of teaching manuals, and all the old embossed books and documents relating to their past use were put to the flames in the courtyard. That done, the Administrator-Director wrote a review of the systems he had studied for the eyes of the Committee and the Ministry officials. This work roamed over all that had been presented as alternative to the past method used. *Not once was the name Braille mentioned.*

This patent omission offended users and supporters of the Braille code in the institute. The blind genius hid his hurt and continued his quiet pursuit of extending the use of the six-dot pattern, while students persisted in applying the code to their daily work, knowing all the time (one pupil afterwards revealed) that detection by Dufau could result in a thrashing, or a day or two locked in a cupboard on bread and water.

Punishment could not suppress the "domino six" system, and this so impressed the new Deputy Director, Joseph Gaudet, that he decided to learn the Braille code to fathom its secret appeal to the "diminished children". He became the first sighted person able to read and write Braille, and this had far-reaching effects. Through the agency of the friend whom he had appointed as his deputy, Dufau's opposition to Braille would be crushed, and the blind children would win the war. The last battle was to be staged at the inauguration of their grand new Paris home.

A new future opened for the chosen blind children of France, for the nation began to redress age-old neglect and rejection. By Christmas 1843, decades of deprivation and subsistence in the seeping ex-seminary were ended, when, some four years after the first stone had been set, a grand new building stood ready on the site off the Boulevard des Invalides. Imposing, solidly impressive, with a stone facade and arched entrance, the building was set back behind an expansive courtyard, flanked with lawns and garden beds enclosed by gilt-topped iron railings. This was the new home of the Institut Royale des Jeunes Aveugles. What would be done here would change the future for the blind. Through the arched entrance some hundred thousand sight-impaired young people would emerge to face life with confidence, and with the capacity to make their contribution to society. And in the spacious rooms official recognition of Louis Braille's six-dot code would be finally won.

The new life for the inmates of the institute opened on a wintry December day, when they were lifted with their few possessions from the old building on Rue St-Victor. Yet it was not a joyous departure. Blind teachers and senior students alike felt sadness. Some even wept at leaving surroundings in which they had spent the bulk of their lives. They had acquired knowledge, known companionship and found a modicum of security among these mildewed walls and twisting corridors. It was as though they were loath to leave what they knew for something that was strange, no matter how grand! The feeling of loss was so manifest that Gabriel Gauthier gave it musical expression. He wrote a valedictory air, with a farewell chorus, and organised a small choir of blind teachers and students to sing the words at assembly points that had been dominant in their lives: refectory, dormitory, chapel, music-room, workshops, and, in the covered courtyard, by the wall where Vincent de Paul once walked to take alms to prisoners in the tower.

The pain of parting, however, would soon vanish in the thrill of a new home, seeming at first like a puzzling paradise, with unfamiliar straight corridors, feet clacking on floors of polished wood, echoes from high ceilings and marbled staircases, and, with the new sounds, new smells; fresh air from wide windows, pungency of newly painted walls, the sweet-oil scent of new wood, in panelling, settles in the concert hall, desks in the classrooms, and from polished pews in the chapel, with its domed roof, which the Abbot from

St-Nicolas-du-Chardonnet seminary blessed on Christmas Eve 1843, fifty-seven years to the day after Valentin Haüy's first blind children had performed at the Palace of Versailles before the ill-fated King Louis XVI and Queen Marie Antoinette.

And there were unaccustomed luxuries; a multiple bathroom with metal tubs, and water faucets attached, which they were allowed to use twice every month, the well-equipped kitchen with a trained staff, whence came each day tempting aromas of a variety of dishes never known in the old St-Firmin Seminary galley. The memory of the years spent in that place of "foul emanations" soon began to dwindle. Dufau spoke of those times in the new assembly hall:

Some of us remember clearly when this institute was housed in premises so unfortunately assigned—and they will not easily forget the classrooms, workshops, sunless dormitories, the corridors, narrow and damp, a place where certain maladies were almost endemic, all of them miseries accumulated under the influence of a fatal discouragement that was not sufficiently combatted . . .

If his words blamed his predecessor he did not name him, any more than he had named the six-dot code in his review of writing systems for the blind. The obliteration of that system would not long be maintained, however, and his own friend, the man he had appointed to occupy the position from which he had plotted to displace the previous Director, would cause drastic change.

The Administrator-Director, in the euphoria of the new home and his new importance, made other changes and arrangements. No longer would there be strict segregation of the sexes. The boys were allowed to know that there were blind girls in the same building, although classes were still held separately. Also, Dufau planned a great day of inauguration, and invitations went out to celebrities of Parisian life: leaders in Government and the church, nobles from the royal court, the faculties, members of the Chamber of Deputies, publishers and the media. It was planned as a grand opening. For the future blind children of France, and those beyond the seas, it would be a remarkable event.

Joseph Gaudet, by then a firm convert to the use of Braille's systems for writing language and music, could not let the opportunity slip. To argue the compelling advantages of the six-dot code, he decided to appeal to reason, to defeat prejudice and bigotry. He secretly wrote a sixteen-page pamphlet, headed *An Account of the System of Raised Dots for use of the Blind*, and had it printed only days prior to the inauguration ceremony, held on 22 February 1844, when the notables crowded the assembly hall to hear Dufau claim:

France was the first country to be moved by richly deserved sympathy for the blind! This nation endowed modern civilisation with the method and means for education of sightless children. It has now provided them with living conditions so improved as to open to them a future without limit.

The prayers, music, speeches over, Joseph

Gaudet staged an exhibition of Louis Braille's six-dot system. His pamphlet placed in the hands of important persons of influence, he brought in a blind boy, equipped with Braille board and stylus, and had a member of the audience read lines chosen at random from a book; he took the imprinted paper from the boy and a blind girl came into the hall to finger-read what had been written.

This was done with words and with music. And the astonished gathering broke into warm applause and congratulations for the boys and girls, and for Dufau and Gaudet. The blind genius himself sat quiet, unnamed and unnoticed, in a row of blind teachers, hearing the only public acclaim that would reach his ears. The proof was inescapable. The speed and facility shown by the blind pupils banished doubt and distrust, abolished bigotry and made it inevitable that the irresistible force of genius behind the six simple dots would triumph in the minds of sighted men and women.

Before long, Dufau could relate how his "diminished children" would sit in class and write with stylus and board, "just as sighted pupils do with pens and pencils". He introduced a new prize to the annual awards: for writing and reading Braille! In a few years he would glory in the fact of the institution he controlled being the birthplace of one of the greatest benefactions the world's blind people would know. In the meantime the body of work in Braille was gradually increased, but only in the Paris institute. Not until later, too late to bring a glow to the heart of Louis Braille, was the word to spread abroad, throughout France and across the world, through the agency of the man they would call the Apostle of Braille, Joseph Gaudet. Prayers, poetry, the scriptural story, The Way of the Cross and then the periodical he founded, edited, and published: *Teacher of the Blind*. From his work, examples of Braille went out in many languages, English, Spanish, German, Italian, even Latin, to influence blind schools that had sprung up in most capitals. And Joseph Gaudet would then assert that the system would have vanished, along with the name of the creator, had it been left to Louis Braille! "He was far too modest, too withdrawn to insist on the rightful place for his code in the life of the blind. We had to do it for him! We had to make his work and his name known outside the institution."

Gaudet had not spent twenty-five critical years of his life in the place of misery on Rue St-Victor. Gaudet had not emerged from that stink of foul air with the mark of death on him. He had his vigour, his sight and power that had never come to the blind village boy who had sat under a tree while the inspiration of genius touched his mind. When Gaudet made his first breach into the age-old wall of indifference and unconcern, Louis Braille was sick, growing frail. Even then, his work was not finished, and his life was yet to be rounded out and his faith uplifted by a new association with spirituality.

Louis Braille was now thirty-five years old. He could not endure long days in classrooms, with the burden of individual coaching, teaching, instruction. Bending over books and boards, guiding fingers to read, left him faint and dizzy. Dufau excused him from those chores and allowed him to concentrate on teaching music, training students for the organ, cello and piano. Even so, each day he would haul his thin frame up three flights of stairs to his room—his sanctuary of rest —the only room he ever had entirely for his own private use. The privacy was sorely needed. In that room he would be forced to spend days resting; in that room he suffered again a gush of blood from his lungs, and yet again. But he remained calm; he rested, and he took up his work once more. He embarked on the biggest single expense of his life. He drew out a third of his savings—compulsorily stopped from his meagre teaching salary—and bought a piano. After that, with his ailing friend Gauthier, he knew happy hours in his room, transcribing great music to Braille notation and playing what Gauthier had written.

On some days the inventive Foucault came to discuss how they might further improve the Piston Board method of writing, so that more blind people could use it. Neither of them were completely satisfied that they had perfected the board, but the problems seemed at times insuperable. Foucault later set down the situation as they saw it:

278

The mechanics of the piston board device could not come easily to people who had been made blind later in life. For them, manipulation of the board was more difficult than using a pen or pencil with a guide to form letters. Something different, some new approach was needed. We wanted an instrument that would suit the needs of *all* blind people! We felt a need for something that the blind could use to write to sighted people without having to study and to learn something which, if they knew the alphabet, and how to spell, they could just sit down and use.

Foucault went away after his times with Louis Braille with ideas buzzing in his mind, his talent challenged to build another bridge to increase contact between the blind and sighted people.

When summer bloomed in 1844, Louis Braille found new pleasure in his private room. He could leave the wide windows open and hear the life of the city. On the morning air the noisy clack of iron wheels on the new railway lines would come clear, and there would be scurrying feet, the clatter of hooves, the sound of carriage wheels on the cobbles; and a new picture for his mind to conjure, yet another strange noise indicating the emerging industrial change, the distinctive noise of steamboats chugging along the river.

One day that summer change came into the subdued tempo of his life, with an offer he could not, and would not, turn away so long as his legs would carry him. A senior priest of the Lazarite movement came to offer him the organ at the new Lazarite chapel, recently built along Rue de Sèvres, the street that ran beside the institute. Louis Braille, no longer active as a teacher, more an honoured figure in the new building than part of the normal teaching staff, still held his reputation as a brilliant instrumentalist, performing with that special clarity of expression he had learned in his youth under the guidance of the masters from the Conservatorium. The Lazarists wanted him at their organ, not a remarkable instrument, one that would later be replaced by a noted builder of church organs, Cavaillé-Coll. It was not the quality of the temporary instrument that drew the ailing blind man, nor the proximity of the chapel to his room, for he still needed a sighted pupil to be his "little guide" to help him trudge the distance. What impelled him to draw on the last of his strength to walk the street and play for hours at a time was that the chapel was sanctified. It was the place where they had finally laid St. Vincent de Paul to rest.

That fact was soothing to Louis Braille's soul; it brought ease to a mind troubled by dark thoughts of impending death. The presence of the relic of the great patron saint of charity, historian Pierre Henri would write, "brought shelter and inspiration". There was for him here the affinity of the legend of boyhood, of knowing during his first days at the old St-Firmin Seminary that he walked where the saint had trod, that the saint had also prayed in the same dowdy chapel. And now, in this hall of worship, he could feel the warm glow of the saint's spirit presence. It would never have been in Louis Braille's nature to have seen any similarity between his own life and that of Vincent de Paul, their common rural beginnings and lives given to the service of others to ease affliction and poverty. Yet, it was there.

Louis Braille could draw inspiration from being able to run his fingers across the organ keys and know that only yards away there rested the beautiful silver reliquary in which the body of the saint had been encapsuled; but not all the body. When the great man died in 1660, he had been entombed in the mother-house of the Sisters of Charity, and when the time came to move his remains to the priory at St-Lazare, the nuns had his heart removed and kept it as a precious relic, at the chapel in the Rue du Bac. Minus heart, the sanctified cadaver had been shifted several times during the revolution, to escape vandalism. The place of worship at St-Lazare had been pillaged and turned into a prison to hold "enemies of the People". Finally the casket had rested within the stone walls of Notre-Dame de Paris and had been brought to the new chapel on Rue de Sèvres when Louis Braille was just twenty-one years old. The seed of belief sowed in his young mind by the former Benedictine monk, the faith that had grown within him across the frugal years, the ache for some permanence to his being came to fruition in this setting of holy music and human charity. Here the words could come to his mind, in a life of darkness, with comforting realism, "I am the Way, the Truth, and the Light", and would uplift his spirit.

Among his contemporaries at the institute it seemed his manner took on a new softness, a readiness to offer sympathy and compassion out of selfless concern. His friends experienced a moral presence when conversing with him; gone was the terse phrase, the seeking of the concise utterance. He seemed to have grasped a universal truth, of the power of love and charity, and this quality shone from his drawn face. His friend, Hippolyte Coltat, commented on this:

He did not limit himself to soothing, kindly words. He joined action to his devotion so as to be useful and to succour the unfortunate. He concealed his own part in the inventions from those who received them and he did these things with simplicity and delicacy. It was not enough just to give. For

283

him the giving was in the Christian spirit of Charity, with respect for the human soul. It was this nobility of sentiment that he brought to the practice of his lively and solid faith which was profound.

There was also regular contact with Dr. Pignier during these times of trial, and the dismissed Director noted how Louis Braille's correspondence and actions were "full of charity". He wrote in his chronicle of Braille's life:

Using great discretion, he carried out many acts of charity, and he never talked about the good he was able to do. Many of his deeds were not known until after his death, when, to the surprise of his closest friends, it was discovered that he had little money, that he had not invested his salaries in some area of high interest. On the contrary, he had invested where it did the greatest good. He invested in God's work. He paid for books, for boards and equipment, for his poor students. He paid for his own writing machines—and he lived a very frugal life. He won a happy disposition by this which helped him until the hour he died.

If there was a reward for this pious charity it came in the last hours of life.

Four years of driving his inventive talent to the limit brought the blinded Foucault to supreme achievement. From assiduous application he was able to carry his machine into the Paris institute one day in late summer of 1847 and proudly hand it to Louis Braille, the genius to whom he owed, and acknowledged, his inspiration. He called his apparatus a Keyboard Printer. It had grown out of discussion with Braille, out of his own talent and technical gifts, out of years of trial and error and redesigning of parts, and it was the forerunner of the typewriter that, in future times, blind writers would use in a hundred lands. It was indeed a prototype of Braille computer keyboards, which would come into use more than a century hence.

A delighted Louis Braille ran sensitive fingers over and across the machine, and was touched with wonder at what had been created. His fingertips on the keys would have taken his mind back to his boyhood, when first in the institute, to tracing raised letters in the heavy old embossed books that were the legacy of Valentin Haüy's days. There were two, parallel keyboards on Foucault's invention. Each held thirty keys, a total of sixty, with raised letters, punctuation marks, accents and numerals; all enlarged and raised enough for the most insensitive touch. Intersecting the two keyboards was a leather tag, which gave the spacing required after each completed word. When each key was pressed by the finger, the type-face impacted downwards onto a platen surface, striking tracing paper into a sharp black print and impressing on the rag paper the same shape of letter.

They had crossed the gulf between blind and sighted writers and Foucault could later proudly explain:

The piston board device was useful, but only as far as it went. We realised that it was difficult for people who had gone blind later in life than we had. It did not help much those who had been used to writing with pen or pencil. So, we wanted a machine that would suit *all* blind people. We needed an instrument with which they could all write, immediately, without training or the need to practise for a long time. I worked to overcome this problem, and though I made many mistakes on the way, I think we won through with the keyboard printer.

Foucault boasted of his own speed with the keyboard. He said he had been able to write 70 verses of Alexandran poetry in a single hour, and that with regular use he would attain even greater speed.

I hope, and believe, that with this keyboard printer blind people, and those who can see as well, will be able to write as quickly as they can with a pen. More importantly it means that blind people will be able to record easily their ideas and thoughts on paper, provided they know the alphabet and how to spell.

287

And for those who would be taught only the Braille alphabet the keys could easily be changed from raised letters to symbols of the six-dot code.

For Louis Braille the invention was a heartening advance during a summer of illness. The weeks had been marked by flushes of bleeding from his lungs, by many days of resting with the taste of blood in his mouth, idle days broken only by his weekly pilgrimage to play the organ in the Lazarite chapel. He did not go for his annual sojourn in Coupvray that summer. Late in September, having acquired facility with Foucault's Keyboard Printer, he used it to write a letter to his mother, hiding his serious condition, but displaying the tug on his mind that the thought of home always evoked in him. The form of the letter would have surprised the 80–year-old Madame Monique Braille. In place of the spidery scrawl of the blinded man's hand using a pen, here was a script, perfectly formed, regular, even—just as though it had been printed by machine! The heading was clear, sharp, black:

"*Ma chére Maman . . .*"

He told how he had wanted to spend a

week with her, at least, but would have to put off his visit if the weather was not good. And he added: "I feel I want to see you very much, for, staying here in the big city is very wearing for me and I would be so happy to breathe again our good country air and to stroll with you in the vineyard."

There was delight in the thought that he might again be with his family, whom he had not visited for more than a year, and he remembered his sister and her children and the orphaned Marienesse children and his godchild, Louise, and he closed: "My dear Mother, please receive, once again, your respectful son's affection."

There was no hint of days spent in the institute infirmary being nursed back from bleeding attacks, nothing of the bodily weakening that bent his thoughts towards retiring, no clue to the strength he drew from hours at the organ of the Lazarite chapel and the uplifting of the soul from the near presence of the remains of the supreme examplar of human charity and courage, St. Vincent de Paul.

Hard times struck again at the poor people

of France. The dreaded potato disease, which caused famine in Ireland, had spread through Europe and caused hunger in rural homes, and aroused discontent, which led to upheavals in national politics. Rising unemployment and bitter winter weather added to unrest and shook the reign of Louis-Philippe to its foundations. Late in February 1848 inmates of the institution on Boulevard des Invalides could hear angry mobs chanting as they marched in protest through the streets. Victor Hugo would write of the clash that brought sudden violence down on the city that month, of the regiment of *cuirassiers* firing in panic into a marching crowd:

Eighty dead and wounded remained on the site. A universal cry of horror and fury arose—"Vengeance!" The bodies were loaded on a cart lit with torches. The cortège moved back, at funeral pace, amid curses. In a few hours Paris was covered with barricades.

On the following afternoon the nerve of the aged Louis-Philippe fell away, and he abdicated. So ended the July Monarchy, and the door was open to the Second Republic, and, consequently, to the Second Empire.

In these dramatic weeks Louis Braille suffered what Coltat described as "a further accident". This attack was so severe that it disturbed Dufau and Gaudet into persuading Braille that he would benefit from some further months of enforced leave (without pay) in the clean air of his home village, where he could rest and regain some of his strength. With the first suggestion of spring 1848 he left the infirmary and travelled to the Brie village to spend the months of summer with his mother and family. He was content at first to rest and idle his days away and, when the sun grew stronger, to visit friends and relatives, to play a game of whist called "Boston" with embossed patterns on the cards, and dominoes with his brother.

The months slipped away without further loss of blood. He ate well, rested, basked in the August sun and gained the feeling of returning health, so that his thoughts turned compellingly to his work at the institute, to his pupils and fellow teachers. The call of duty grew too strong to resist. In early September he was on the stage coach out of Meaux, rolling over the hard road to a Paris scarred by street battles fought against royalist troops by thousands of angry, hungry, unemployed, many of whom had since been transported to North Africa. Revolution was in the air again, with memories of the Terror. The desire for "authority" turned eyes towards the figure of Louis Napoleon, waiting on the sidelines for destiny's call.

Amid daily news of riots, political demonstrations, charges of corruption in high places, Louis Braille resumed a moderated daily schedule. The illusion of a return to health soon fell away, and illness sharpened again the nostalgia for his village home. In the third week of November he went again to Foucault's Keyboard Printer and wrote to his mother: "It is six weeks since I left you and in that long time I have had no word from you. Will you please write and tell me that you are well, and give the news of our family, all our relatives, and those friends who may sometimes speak of me to you . . ."

The windows of his third-storey room were shut against winter air and snow showers, but as he tapped away on the Keyboard Printer, he could still hear the boom of artillery rolling across the city. Salvoes were being fired to celebrate the adoption of the Constitution of the Second Republic. With his thoughts back in the village of his birth, strolling with his mother with the sun on his face in the family vineyard, he wrote:

I noticed with satisfaction, Mother, how the weather was fine during the time for harvesting the grapes—big, beautiful as one could wish, I hope. Today, here, the sun is absent and the bad weather is beginning. So, Mother, you must stay inside. As for me, I do not go out. While Parisians are outdoors and getting snow on their heads celebrating the Constitution, I am happy to stay in my warm little room and listen to them firing the cannon.

There was hint of his struggle in his final paragraph and an expectation that would not be met.

We must continue to be brave, Mother.

We must get through this coming winter, after which I hope to be with you again. Until that happy time, be assured once more of your loving son's affection . . .

He would be brave, nobly courageous, in the ordeal that lay ahead of him, but he would never again stroll with his mother in the family vineyard.

Louis Braille had lived his life under dramatic changes of fortunes for France and a string of different regimes. In boyhood there had been the decline and fall of Napoleon's First Empire, which had brought the voices and boots of foreigners into his home; he had known the distant royal interest in youth of the portly King Louis XVIII and the continuation of the restoration of the Bourbon monarchy with Charles X and its final demise; then had come the Orleanist monarch Louis-Philippe, whose greatest glory in Louis Braille's mind was that his reign coincided with not only a new home for the blind children, but also an awakening of concern for the sightless.

Louis-Philippe's July Monarchy had ended in abdication, and the Second Republic had been enforced with its Constitution under the presidency of the ambitious Louis Napoleon, nephew to the great man who was now a legend of authority and whose corpse had been brought back from St. Helena to lie in honour among the nation's heroes.

Louis Braille, too wasted to stand on his own feet, invalided to the institute's infirmary, heard that the wheel of destiny had turned full circle, how on this second day of December 1851—selected specially for the forty-sixth anniversary of the battle of Austerlitz—there had been a *coup d'état* to put another Napoleon on the throne of France. Louis Napoleon was to take France into a Second Empire. In his life's work and writing Louis Braille had never involved himself in arguments on politics or national affairs. With his spirit of compassion and charity he leaned to the appeal of equality, fraternity, liberty, yet his father's support of royalty was still strong in his mind. Lying in his bed in the infirmary, he could discuss these matters with friends when they visited him, particularly with Gabriel Gauthier. The blind composer left no record of these talks, except to relate some exchanges to Dr. Pignier, who recorded a memorable statement. Braille had said: "God has granted me favours. I am happy to have done something that might ease the lot of those whose misfortune we share. This illness has done my soul good. So, talk to me about God, dear friend."

The confidences between them would have been poignant. Two blinded teachers, unburdening their minds to each other, both facing inevitable death from the same implacable infection, and both assured, certain, and unafraid in the comfort their faith gave them. Gauthier still had the strength to embrace his companion in life —and death—and to go to his room to write his last music, a homage that would be a paean of praise for his dying friend.

On 4 December 1851—two days after the *coup* that put a Napoleon back on the throne of France—Louis Braille suffered an attack of bleeding that Coltat would describe as a "formidable blow", a surge of blood and tissue that, he recorded, "frightened those who attended the patient. Yet Louis Braille retained his profound calm and, knowing his life was closing, asked for spiritual aid and received the sacraments from the visiting priest, with piety."

When Hippolyte Coltat came to see him the day after this tender ministration, Louis Braille's voice was weak almost to a whisper, but his tone was elated, his wan, drawn face near to beaming. Coltat wrote every halting word the dying man spoke. After forty years in total blindness, a glorious radiance of heavenly light had come to his vision. He said:

Yesterday was the most beautiful and greatest day of my life. Oh, the unfathomable mystery of the human heart! Yesterday I tasted supreme delight. God deigned to show me— shining before my eyes—the glory of eternal hope. And to experience *that* is to understand the majesty and the power of religion.

Coltat wrote the words down "to be conserved as a priceless treasure". And his writing shows that Braille spoke further:

I am convinced my mission on earth is done. After that, surely, there is nothing capable of attaching me to this life any longer. Well, I have been asking God to take me from this world. That is true. But, I feel perhaps I have not been asking loudly enough.

His call was answered, but not quickly. His life's blood passed through his mouth again, and again, and it was as though his spirit would not release his soul. He lingered on, day after day, though he had been given extreme unction. Dreamily, in his illness, he passed through the days of Christmas and into the new year, which seemed to bring another partial return of strength. In that delusion he dictated his will to a notary and placed his earthly affairs in the hands of Hippolyte Coltat, as his executor. He lived on still, past his forty-third birthday and finally came to 6 January 1852, to Epiphany, and he remembered this was the day to recall the manifestation of Jesus Christ to the Magi. Coltat recorded:

He asked to be reminded of the

symbolic meaning of the gold, incense, and myrrh the three Kings presented to Him whose star they had seen shining in the East. Around noon, feeling the end close, he asked for communion and received the holy bread with touching piety to fortify himself for the fearful passage.

Late that afternoon, candles were lit, and in their wavering light people came to take a last farewell. There were fellow teachers, sighted and blind, and priests from the Lazarite chapel and St-Nicolas-du-Chardonnet, where he had made his first communion and had been confirmed. Dufau and Gaudet stood by, and also present was Dr. Pignier, who would write how he "received the last breath of both Louis Braille and Gabriel Gauthier, my dear children". The only relative present was Louis-Simon, and Coltat recorded how the two brothers embraced in those last hours:

Louis Braille gave to each person the most touching signs of affection. When he was no longer able to speak, his lips formed silent movements of tenderness more eloquent than any words, and all present were moved to tears. His agony started at four in the afternoon and at seven-thirty, on the evening of Epiphany, Louis Braille placed his beautiful soul in the hands of God.

That evening, along the boulevard by the river, there were celebrations. Crowds sang songs of triumph, lit fires, exploded fireworks, sent rockets soaring into the January night, rejoicing that another Napoleon was on the throne of France. A palace banquet was held under glittering crystal chandeliers, with the elated nephew of the great Emperor surrounded by colourfully dressed nobles and bejewelled women. Louis Braille, whose name would outlast and transcend them all, died, unknown outside the institute, unremarked by the people of Paris, indeed, unknown to the world at large.

Requiem mass was to be held in the chapel where Louis Braille had played the organ and prayed, beneath an arch with a mural of Christ holding out a hand in benediction with the words: *"And the eyes of the Blind will move out of the night towards the Light.*" But, first, Administrator-Director Dufau had formalities to complete. He had been handed a sum of more than 1200 francs, collected spontaneously among friends, pupils, blind teachers, priests, for a suitable memorial of remembrance of Louis Braille. Compelled now to accept Dr. Pignier's protégé as an honoured figure in the history of the institute, Dufau called in the sculptor Jouffroy to prepare for a bust of the dead man to be cut from a block of marble he would obtain from the Ministry. Jouffroy took a plaster cast for the head. The cast would remain in the institute, where over the decades the features would be explored by the fingers of tens of thousands of blind pupils. Both Dufau and Jouffroy were sighted men. It did not occur to them to take a cast of the hands that arguably would be among the most fascinating in human history, and which had delivered blessings on the blind.

A saddened Hippolyte Coltat found himself with Louis Braille's life-savings and possessions to distribute according to the dictated wishes. There was a total sum of 585 francs, to which was added 250 francs from the sale of Braille's beloved piano. Artefacts, books, writing boards, machines were all to go to relatives and friends, and the land he had inherited from his father was to remain in the family, while his mother was to receive 300 francs so that she would not have to sell the cottage in order to live. There was a sum of 292 francs for a committee organising employment for blind pupils, and the rest of the gifts were tiny sums of touching memory. There were sums of 40 francs for the Lazarists and the curé of Coupvray, for saying masses for the repose of his soul; there were small gifts for the Congregation of St-Nicolas-du-Chardonnet, for his "little guide", the infirmary nurse, and the lady who cleaned his room. There was also an additional sum of 60 francs to help print books with raised dots.

With formalities completed, Dufau released the body to Louis-Simon, who hired a horse and cart along Rue de Grenelle and drove for seven hours over the rough road to Coupvray, with the coffin bumping in the back. On the morning of 10 January 1852, in the old graveyard on top of the village hill, with bare trees stabbing a wintry sky, they lowered the wooden casket into a simple grave, with only Monique Braille, her family and a few friends standing by.

Beneath a slab of rough-cut granite that would be darkened by many winters and invaded by green mould, Louis Braille's remains rested undisturbed while tumultuous history rolled back and forth across France and his system of the "domino six" dots flowed quietly to a lasting conquest.

6

Postcript

THROUGH a hundred summers and winters Louis Braille's coffin lay undisturbed beneath the granite slab in a simple grave. In June 1952 there came dozens of grateful pilgrims from around the world eager to join in a belated homage France was to pay to its global benefactor. White sticks tapping an insistent path, they thronged a village seemingly untouched by time, still grey and venerable as the old church on the hill, as full of historical reverie as it was in the days after the Russian occupation troops marched away and the King was back on the throne. No hint here of dramas unfolded in that century, no sign of four foreign invasions, no scars from giant shells the Huns had fired from the banks of the Marne into Paris, not a trace of the tracks of Nazi Panzers on the cobbles, nor of the Allied columns on their way to victory in the east. Only a change or two for these sightless wayfarers: the statue, based on Jouffroy's death mask, standing in the square now named for Braille, the bas-relief that exploring fingers could read; and a marble plaque attached to the crumbling wall of the old cottage in the Chemin des Buttes, which read to them by sighted guides announced: "He opened the door to knowledge for all those who cannot see."

Rusted horseshoes were still nailed over the side door; the tackle Simon-René had used to haul bags of wheat and barley flour to the attic was in place, and still mounted on the front wall was the iron arm that once carried the sign: BOURRELIER—BRAILLE. The blind pilgrims found wonderment in this 300-year-old home; standing in the workroom with the saddler's tools over the bench where historical blindness occurred; feeling wooden panels in the recess where the sickly child was delivered; running hands along the wooden rail where the boy Louis climbed the stairs to sleep under the roof; tracing the nailed letters of the alphabet in strips of wood. By following the curved rough stone wall through clumps of butter-cups they came to the place where the youthful genius had sat under a tree "pinpricking" sheets of paper with his father's awl on his way to immortality.

Touched by this moment, the gifted Helen Keller wrote to mark this place: "Here, by genius and kindness, woven into the life of Louis Braille, a new ray of light penetrated the world of the blind."

There was yet the supreme moment for the intrepid blind travellers: up the steeply cobbled La Touarte, across the square to the crumbling graveyard under the aged shoulder of the church, there to stand with breezes of the soft Brie country stirring thick-leaved beeches, by a plain slab of granite distinguished only by a slim rusting cross embossed with a small face with closed eyes. Chisel-cut words in the granite said there rested beneath a "teacher at the Institute for Blind Children, inventor of the raised point system of writing". The words—almost inde-cipherable from the grime and mould of the century—were partly covered by a single tribute, a weather-worn garland of painted aluminium with a fading inscription, in English: "With the gratitude of all blind people to their illustrious benefactor —25 July 1937."

That was the year when blind citizens of Paris had planned to fund a statue to be erected at some notable city road-junction, a plan that was dropped with the threat of war from Nazi Germany. Now, at the graveside on 20 June 1952, France, and time, were to atone for long neglect and indifference. Sighted officials, empowered with the authority of the National Assembly, acted to endow honour to the nation's most famous blind man. They opened the grave and lifted the soil-encrusted wooden casket, which had bumped its way from Paris in 1852, and which held the bones of a man whose family name had become a household word around the globe.

They prised open the lid of his coffin. It was planned that these revered remains would make the terminal journey west, through Lagny to the metropolis, to lie in honour—not a stone's throw from where he had spent his adult life—in the hallowed hall of the Panthéon, that former church with a soaring dome that had been converted during the Revolution to "house the relics of the great men of the days of French freedom". There Braille would be honoured together with Voltaire, Victor Hugo, Mirabeau, Rousseau, Emile Zola, and many others.

But—wait! It was all very well for Paris to make decisions, but what would there be left for the commune of Coupvray? A cottage that might be a small museum—a statue—an empty grave? This soil had bred Braille; here his people had lived for three centuries; here he was born and registered, christened and baptised! In this village he went to school and learned the alphabet; here he had rested for one hundred forgotten years! So, what would there be left for the place of his birth? *Le Maire* was insistent and eloquent, and authority yielded. The stately cortège left Coupvray, with its escort of Republic Guards, and followed by the blind devotees; but, just as Vincent de Paul had been laid in his final home minus his heart, so Louis Braille went back to Paris, his body incomplete. The hands that had written the first dots of the Braille code had been separated from his skeleton. The bones had been encased in a small concrete container, little bigger than a shoe-box, held together with iron bolts.

On the day the cortège left Coupvray, a religious service was held over the empty grave, the granite slab replaced, and the concrete container bolted to the surface with the inscription: "The Commune of Coupvray piously keeps in this urn the hands of the genius inventor Louis Braille."

The commemorations in Paris lasted the weekend. Louis Braille was first carried into the building where he had died—now the National Institute for Blind Juveniles —and his shining new reliquary was set on a catafalque adorned with floral tributes that came from far and wide. Blind students and teachers kept vigil through to the dawning of Sunday, 22 June. The casket was then taken into the forecourt and placed beneath the statue of Valentin Haüy and his first blind pupil, François Lesueur, so Parisians who had gathered could also pay homage. Soon after nine that morning it was taken in convoy through streets Louis Braille had walked in life to play the organ in some famous church, finally to reach the square in front of the Panthéon, where the President of France, M. Vincent Auriol, waited to salute the cortège as the Guards' Band played the Marseillaise. The coffin, overlain with the tricolour of France, was taken into the nave.

Next morning *Le Figaro* told Parisians:

Oh, what a touching, heart-moving procession! The columns of blinded people—children, boys and girls, youths, men and women, elderly folk, people from more than twenty different lands—walking with descendants of the Braille family, with the staff and teachers of the blind institute, past the columns of Republic Guards in their resplendent uniforms, to where a giant flag is draped from the high dome.

Speeches and messages of tribute expressed the homage—from the Secretary-General of the United Nations, Trygve Lie, and from many national leaders; and the French Minister of Health, M. Ribeyre, named Louis Braille as the "conqueror of eternal night". They carried him down winding stone stairs to below the main hall, to a vault off the echoing crypt, to rest behind a barred gate with three other notables—all scientists—Paul Langevin, physicist, prisoner of the Nazis, whose name had been linked in an affair of the heart with the widowed Marie Curie; also mentor to Frederic Joliot-Curie, her son-in-law, Langevin had died in 1946! There also is Paul Painlevé, mathematician and politician, died 1933; and the only woman in the crypt, Sophie Bertholet, pioneer physicist, who died in 1907.

That same time there was a mass at Notre-Dame cathedral, where blind pupils of the institute formed the choir, and also a ceremony at the Sorbonne, where Helen Keller was the speaker. Months later a conference was held of blind people in the southern port city of Marseilles, and there author and historian Henri Gauvrit spoke of Braille's work and how his code had "encircled the world", when UNESCO in 1949 had taken a hand to spread international benefits of the system to a hundred countries, to such languages as Arabic, Hindu and Chinese, and into

311

hundreds of dialects. He spoke also of the centuries of dispassion and neglect of the sightless, and added:

And then came light for the blind! Braille's six dots worked the miracle. Six wonderful dots, which without the power of prestige, with intrigue imposed on them by authorities in Paris, had the irresistible force of genius and the long-contained power of a class of human beings possessed of the desire for life, of the need to mingle in the mainstream of society . . .

From Paris the wonderful dots set out, against long and prejudiced opposition, to conquer Europe. They had to win in the end and there came the first great international victory, at the World Congress for the Blind, in Paris in 1878, and one after another countries came to adopt the six dots as the proper means of writing and reading for the blind. Of all these western countries, however, it was the United States of America that held out. Then, at last, in 1917, the 48 stars and the stripes of America capitulated before the six marvellous dots.

312

7

The Braille Benefaction

BLINDNESS is a universal affliction. Problems that attend a life of darkness admit no barriers of colour, creed or race. This is why the genius of Louis Braille, born when the military power of France was at peak, could peacefully cross the world's frontiers into lands Napoleon's imperial eagles could never reach. Products of the talent in that blind village lad are now known in every corner of his earth, and his name is synonymous with the alleviation of suffering, of service to humanity, of a scope few benefactors have achieved.

In the far-off Chinese city of Canton his genius touched the life of a young girl blinded by the ministrations of a travelling mendicant. Lucy Ching, happily, had a family amah and this unusual servant knew Braille and taught her charge to read and write. Lucy grew up to make her

313

mark as author and eminent social worker in the teeming streets of Hong Kong.

Famous Irish-born flautist James Galway, while in Spain, performed a beautiful Fantasia, written for him by blind composer Rodrigo on his Braille typewriter. At the same time, in the same country, José Feliciano rehearsed music with Braille notation.

On the Indian subcontinent, in Lahore, a blind boy was admitted to the St. Dunstan's home for blinded soldiers at the behest of Lady Mountbatten, and was there taught to read, write—and type—Braille. Today Ved Mehta leads a busy life, as author and television personality.

In the United States Billy Eckstein, singer-composer, owed development of his talent to Braille music. In the 1985 Academy Awards, blind entertainer and song-writer, Stevie Wonder, found his way amid stunning applause to the Hollywood rostrum to receive his Oscar for the song of the year, "I just called to say I love you". Stevie did not have time to mention his debt to Braille, but it was there, just as it always is when French classical pianist Bernard d'Ascoli gives exquisite

314

performances on the world's concert stages, of works by Chopin, Mendelssohn, Debussy, Bach or Beethoven.

These are a few of the lives Louis Braille's work has touched. Like countless thousands among today's 40 million blind beings, they draw benefit from a triumph over adversity achieved in long illness, and a life of near-penury, which few people know about. Yet the name Braille is known everywhere. As blind historian Pierre Henri wrote, using his own Braille board and stylus: "He is a symbol to the blind of this planet, the man who freed his unfortunate brothers from the old shackles that went with blindness."

When he died in 1852, Louis Braille was unknown beyond the walls of the institute that bred his talent, and which sent him to an early grave! Recognition after death was grindingly slow; and even at the last was grudgingly given. When world opinion forced belated honour, and his bones were lifted from the simple grave on the village hilltop, his life's work, his devotion—long after he might have yielded to illness—had opened doors to treasures of literature and music across the globe. He had become, as Helen Keller would write, "light-bearer to a world of darkness". Yet the resting-place accorded him by sighted authority in the hallowed Panthéon was not among the great men of letters that France has produced: not with Voltaire, Victor Hugo, Emile Zola, but below stairs, down a winding stone staircase, and behind iron bars, in a crypt with three scientists whom nobody could claim were very famous outside Paris.

This view is contentious, perhaps, but it is valid none the less, since it reminds all who can read—with or without Braille's aid—of the superior attitude of sighted administrators, those stubborn souls who, wishing to do only what they thought was right, but not wise enough to grasp that the blind knew what was best for them, gave ground slowly, unwillingly, to ultimate truth. And not just in France!

Johan Wilhelm Klein, in Austria, maintained to the last his objection to the blind having their own alphabet, arguing that it would separate the blind and "close them into their own world with symbols that were not for seeing eyes". The conviction that only the Roman alphabet should be used was widespread, and unyielding, until Joseph Gaudet began his campaign in the mid–1850s, with his journals and writing. It was not until 1873, a century after Valentin Haüy opened the first blind school, that a conference in Leipzig of teachers of the blind discussed the Braille code as a teaching medium. This meeting was remarkable for the controversy it aroused, and there was fierce condemnation of "deserting the normal". Yet seeds were sown. Almost a quarter of a century after Braille died, the teachers met again, in Dresden, and there a majority voted to put Braille's code on trial in their institutes.

Coincident with this development, a British medico was working towards the same end. Dr. Thomas Rhodes Armitage had lost his sight late in his career and, facing the prospect of an empty and useless existence, had found the same spirit of service that had come to Louis Braille. He wrote: "Can't conceive of any occupation so congenial to a blind man of education and leisure as an attempt to advance the education and improve conditions for his fellow sufferers."

With typical resolution, Dr. Armitage took arms against a muddled situation for the blind of Britain. There was no unity in reading codes among the institutes, which had by then been set up in most major cities. The good doctor became a pioneer in self-help. He did not turn to the sighted to lead the way. He formed his own executive council of blind men. He founded the British and Foreign Society for Improving Embossed Literature for the Blind, which grew into the modern Royal National Institute. That first blind council set itself the task of sifting the manifold systems of blind writing and reading that were on offer. They set specifications, which, in their wisdom, called for:

- A method of writing and reading most suited to the needs of blind people.
- A code that could be used in more than one language.
- A method that would also be applied to musical notation.

Their study brought a barrage of propaganda. Sighted inventors, teachers, calligraphists, who believed they knew best, even printers who had cast their own symbols into metal type, all saw the chance of immortality and wealth, and pursued the council with claims to originality.

The Braille code withstood all challenge. The versatility, the adaptability of the beautifully simple system—little changed from the early years when Braille worked towards its perfection—remained, as it does today, unsurpassed. The decision of the British council had undoubted influence on the meeting of the World Congress held in Paris in 1878, when delegates, not only from France and Britain, but also from Denmark, Germany, Austria, Hungary, Holland, Italy, Sweden and Switzerland, voted that Braille should be the accepted code for education of the blind.

There was still the citadel of the United States. The barrier had yet to be breached in an increasingly inventive country, where every few years saw some new system proposed. In New York there was some deference to Braille when the "domino six" pattern was turned on its side! This ingenious move put the "cell" for the touch of the blind two dots high, instead of three, and three dots wide in place of two. It was a typical assumption of the sighted, which ignored the shape of the fingertips, that they were deeper than wider, and that a width of three dots banished much of the flexibility of the six-dot code. As with all other proposals, the new idea was found wanting. Not until a national conference was held in Little Rock in 1912 was ground given to Braille. By 1917 his code had won its way across North America and was being used in so many institutes that Henri Gauvrit could write, in 1952, how Braille's marvellous six dots had "conquered the 48 stars and the stripes of America".

The American victory was a milestone, but true global use of Braille was a world war away. In 1949, when the United Nations threw out a pallid gleam of hope for less fortunate peoples of the world, the newly independent India responded by seeking help for the blind among its teeming millions. It was then that UNESCO took the step of unifying various adaptations of Braille into a single accepted code, which could cover all languages and dialects. The work proved so successful that by 1953 the Organisation could claim the result to be "a fine example of what can be achieved when people of different cultures and differing languages work together for the common good".

The successful World Uniformity Program was achieved in affiliation with other UN bodies (WHO and ILO) and in parallel with the efforts of an original grouping of national bodies, the International Federation of the Blind. In November 1984 these two organisations took a further giant step. Meeting in the Saudi Arabian city of Ryadh, they decided to join forces in an historic decision that brought the blind people of earth under one welfare umbrella, a situation that seemed an impossible dream two centuries earlier. Essential to this global unity, none the less, was the communication code picked out by a blind French youth experimenting with his father's awl on the hilltop in Coupvray. A member of that new—and singular—world body told this writer: "it was Louis Braille's invention of the six-dot code which, by making communication among the blind possible, in fact facilitated

—nay, enabled!—a single international force to come into being to watch over the well-being of all blind human beings."

His code is now as universal as blindness. Global in effect, it has been nerve and sinew to the growth of compassion and understanding started with the education of a blind beggar boy in 1771. The years of work and travail have seen the old attitudes swept away; the sightless no longer huddle in corners, roam highways in pathetic groups seeking succour, no longer are rejected and despised. All that has been changed as dramatically, as impressively, indeed, as the city itself, where the world movement was born; for even as the (now) most famous blind man in history was dying in the building on the Boulevard des Invalides, so another man of exactly the same age, who would live until 1891, was planning the rebirth of Paris. Had he been granted a normal life-span, Louis Braille would have lived through the transformation of the medieval city, when most of its narrow alleys and twisting streets, its fortifications and defensive walls, were swept out of existence.

Baron Georges Haussmann, a forceful

Alsatian, huge in body, had hitched his future to the rising star of Napoleon's nephew—head of the Second Empire—and had been rewarded with the post of Préfect of the Seine. With vision as wide as his girth, he tucked the rebuilding of Paris into his portfolio and gave shape to a concept of grandeur, giving Paris fine boulevards, wide streets, paved walkways shaded by trees. He built 140 kilometres of roadways, with vistas and fountains, promenades and parks, and prescribed the eye-catching style of buildings that private enterprise was allowed to construct along the main thoroughfares. In his orgy of town planning, however, the old eye-sore of the St-Firmin Seminary on Rue St-Victor escaped the wrecking hammers.

Vacated by the blind in 1843, it was allowed to survive another eighty years, being used both as an army barracks and storehouse and auction rooms until in the years after World War I it simply had to come down. A modern post office is believed to occupy the old site, but for both blind pilgrims and sighted wayfarers there is no other clue. No sign, no plaque, marks the spot from where the six-dot code set out to conquer the world of the blind. Happily, there are still mementoes associated with Louis Braille and his boyhood in the village of Coupvray, which can be reached by suburban train from Paris to the Brie town of Esbly, and a walk of some three kilometres.

The old church still sits grey-green on the hilltop, with the original font where the sickly child was baptised; the rusty horsehoes nailed over the cottage door for luck remain in place, as does the iron bar that once held the *bourrelier*'s signboard. The sign itself has long gone, along with the original contents of the Braille home.

When old Monique Braille died, in her mid-eighties, the family sold the old home, with all its contents! The cottage crumbled its way towards prime neglect through the passing years, until it was rescued by the Braille Committee that was set up in 1937 to erect the statue in Paris that never was. The Braille Committee bought it with an injection of overseas funds, subscribed mainly from America. Under the auspices of the Commune of Coupvray, a small museum was set up, furbished as near as could be to what it was like in the days when Simon-René was teaching the alphabet to his blind infant son. There are copies of letters Louis wrote to his mother, some of his equipment, and the work-bench, marked by his brother's brass plate and tools hanging on the wall board, in the room where he was blinded by his own hand. But the most poignant moment the ancient village has to offer is to stand under the trees in the decaying graveyard by the empty grave with its slim, rusting iron cross, to run one's fingers over the rough surface of the small concrete box in which rest the bones of the hands that brought hope, change and enlightenment to people who live in a dark world.

Louis Braille was the great benefactor, but he could only alleviate, and not banish, blindness. Unfortunately, mankind will continue to have its great army of sightless people. Blindness will remain universal: through accident, disease, hereditary factors, genetic slip and mindless misuse of drugs. No matter what surgical marvels, devices and inventions may come in the future, the blind will be always part of humanity, and thus alleviation is very precious. By the sufferings of pioneers today's blinded young have been endowed with a future full of hope. Students at the institute where Braille died, like those in similar establishments throughout the world, gain self-confidence, capability and assertiveness. They can perform in the gymnasium, do acrobatics, play sport, climb mountains; and they can go to the Braille keyboard on the computer, a descendant of the instrument that Braille and blind inventor Foucault produced almost a century and a half ago, and with a keyed printer gain access in Braille to vast stores of knowledge, data, statistics and guidance, which open ways to careers in many fields. They can tap huge libraries and use the treasure houses of great music available in Braille at most of the world's blind institutes.

Life is now so full of challenge and exciting possibilities for blinded students of this modern world that they would surely concur with the words uttered to Helen Keller in Cairo in 1952 by the head of the Egyptian Light of the Blind Society, Sheikh Sawy Shaalem, who declared:

"God gave us Louis Braille."

Acknowledgements

PEOPLE in different corners of the world made this book possible and my grateful thanks extend to them all. It began in the southern Australian city of Melbourne over lunch with Jan Smark Nilsson, long-time family friend, member of the World Council for the Welfare of the Blind and executive director of the Braille and Talking Book Library. What she had to say halted a spoonful of French onion soup half-way to my lips. She had searched the literature for a satisfying full-length account of the life and times of history's most famous blind man. Louis Braille had been dead some 130 years, and there have been only brief sketches, booklets, articles for juveniles published, many perpetuating inaccuracies; but for the fingers of her serious readers there was nothing worth transcribing into the six-dot code. I am happy I tried to fill the gap;

this work has already been translated into Braille for the blind to read.

The accounts made by Braille's contemporaries of the triumph of his spirit over penury and suffering had been left to gather a century of dust in Paris archives: the Bibliothèque Nationale, the collections of the Valentin Haüy Association and in the museum maintained at the modern Institute for the Young Blind on Boulevard des Invalides. The documents—memoirs, letters, speeches, valedictory orations and official reports—proved a treasure that was mined efficiently and tirelessly by the Chief Librarian and Researcher at the Australian Embassy in Paris, Alice Gay, who also trudged the cobbles of Coupvray with me in probing search of memorabilia, local legend and atmosphere. My thanks go out to her as they do to the Rt Hon. E. G. Whitlam, then Australia's Ambassador to UNESCO, and to the European Editor of *Selectiones*, M. Dimi Panitzer, and his research staff, and most specially to Yvonne Fourcade and Glorianne Depondt. Through them I was accorded a generous interview with the aged blind historian Pierre Henri, to whom I offered admiration and thanks. At the Paris institute, the *censeur*, the gifted M. Serge Guillemet, gave of his time to guide me on a comprehensive tour of the building on Boulevard des Invalides, including Louis Braille's bedroom, which is now a dental surgery. He also threw open the records held in the museum established to Braille's memory; and help there with documents and personal records was willingly extended by the curator, M. Cornut-Gentil, and his staff.

In London at the Royal National Institute for the Blind, there was no stinting of effort to help. The establishment that serves some 130,000 sight-impaired people throughout Britain, also served me well, and I am specially obliged to Mrs. Rosemary Kingston for help with reproductions. In London, also, Dr. Nancy Price gave rich insights into the affliction of blindness on a young child.

Illustrations for this work came from many willing sources, and a debt is owed to staff of Bibliothèque Nationale, curator and staff of INJA, the Valentin Haüy Association, Librarian and Staff of the Australian Embassy; staff and editor of

Selectiones and the cultural division of the French Foreign Service—all of Paris. As well, aid was given by the Royal National Institute for the Blind, London; and by the Braille Book Society and Dean Photographics, both of Melbourne, Australia.

In Australia, elucidation and translation of old documents was made available by the kindness of Professeur J. C. Radonett of the Cultural Division of the French Foreign Service, through the French Embassy, in Canberra. Among others— their contributions no less for being last— were the research staff and the Principal Librarian, Catherine Santamaria, of the National Library of Australia, who provided a world data research that was a priceless guide. I also owe debts to Helen Dean, of Melbourne, for illustrations, to Maggie Tipka of Sydney for unflagging support, and also to my wife, Pauline, without whom the writing would still not be completed. I am also much indebted to my publisher, Susan Haynes.

Lennard Bickel

Chronology

1771   Valentin Haüy assumes education of a blind beggar boy.

1773   Haüy invents books with raised Roman alphabet. Opens world's first boarding school for blind children.

1788   Blind pupils display ability before King Louis XVI and Queen Marie Antoinette.

1789   Revolution. Convention dismisses Haüy, assumes control of blind school.

1800   First Consul, Napoleon, commits blind pupils to hospice for blind derelicts.

1806   Haüy flees danger of arrest, goes to Germany, Russia, opens new schools for young blind.

1809   Louis Braille born in village of Coupvray, fourth child of Monique and Simon-René, the local harness-maker.

1812 Child Louis blinded by own hand in father's workshop.

1814 Aristocrat army officer Charles Barbier invents system for phonetic messages for army use at night.

1815 Napoleon exiled. Russian occupying troops billeted on Braille cottage; restored King Louis XVIII has blind school resumed in ex-prison seminary building in Paris.

1816 Louis Braille taught alphabet with nails knocked in wood. Enters village school.

1819 Just ten years old, Braille lodged in Paris institute for blind founded by Haüy, who is now barred from premises.

1821 New Director at blind institute. Haüy admitted for visit, meets Louis Braille. Barbier makes first attempt to interest institute authority in system of raised dots.

1824 Braille among pupils chosen to test Barbier's dotted cards. Evolves own code at age fifteen.

1825 Braille's code used by pupils,

rejected by authorities. Braille shows gift for musical instruments, makes lifelong friendship with Gabriel Gauthier.

1826 Braille converts his simplified code system to musical notation.

1828 Braille appointed full teacher. Perfecting Braille system. Panel of doctors warn of health danger in old building.

1829 32-page booklet, explaining six-dot reading and writing system, written and published by Braille.

1831 Simon-René dies after appealing to Pignier, Director, to be surrogate father.

1832 Paris journal exposes conditions in institute, claims too many children dying.

1834 Braille takes up post as organist in notable church. Teaching and improving original code.

1835 First symptoms of consumption; friend Gauthier also consumptive. Braille starts work on large-scale use of six-dot code for transcription.

1837 First full book in Braille: three

volumes of French history, entirely written and imprinted at institute by blind teachers and pupils— opposes controlling body and Ministry policy.

1838 First public condemnation of conditions for blind children by poet Lamartine in Chamber of Deputies. 1.6 million francs voted for new building.

1839 Braille works with collaborators on first devices for printing Braille.

1840 Director Pignier betrayed by deputy Dufau, sacked for allowing work on history book in Braille. Dufau opponent of six-dot code; burns all previous books, brings in new reading systems. Gaudet, who will be known as an Apostle of Braille, is appointed deputy director.

1841 Braille's health failing; recurrent bleeding; sent for long rest in home village.

1843 Move to new building; Gaudet stages display of Braille to VIPs; Braille offered organist job at chapel where Vincent de Paul's remains are kept. Work begins with colleagues (all blind) on machines to speed up writing Braille in literature and music. Gauthier composes first songs.

1847   Dufau forced to recognise genius of Braille, permits use of system in institute. Braille and Foucault plan design of first Braille "typewriter", called a Keyboard Printer.

1848   Braille suffers disabling attacks of bleeding; can teach music to only a few students. Writes first letters on the Keyboard Printer invention.

1851   Too ill to work; committed to infirmary.

1852   Braille dies 6 January. Family claim body for burial in a plain grave in village.

1856   Gaudet promotes Braille across France; sends collection of prayers in Braille to many countries. Founds new magazine for blind teachers, promoting use of Braille.

1868   British council for blind formed; adopts Braille as code superior to all competitors.

1878   World Congress chooses Braille for blind.

1890   Braille system adopted in blind schools in Germany, Austria, Spain, Scotland, England, Denmark, Belgium.

1917   Modified form of Braille recommended for general use in United States.

1929   Council of ten nations in Paris decide use of Braille for international music notation.

1949   India asks UNESCO to regulate Braille code for use in all languages. World Uniformity Program established bringing codified Braille to a hundred languages and hundreds of dialects.

1952   A century after his death, France recognises Braille as world benefactor. National Assembly orders removal of bones from village to Paris to be kept in Panthéon. 20 June: Coffin raised. Commune claims the hands of the genius inventor to be kept in village. Bones of Braille's hands separated, placed in sealed concrete box on top of the empty tomb. Remainder of body carried for ceremonial burial attended by President of France and blind pilgrims from across the world present with messages of tribute from many world leaders.

GUIDE
TO THE COLOUR CODING
OF
ULVERSCROFT BOOKS

Many of our readers have written to us expressing their appreciation for the way in which our colour coding has assisted them in selecting the Ulverscroft books of their choice.

To remind everyone of our colour coding— this is as follows:

BLACK COVERS
Mysteries

★

BLUE COVERS
Romances

★

RED COVERS
Adventure Suspense and General Fiction

★

ORANGE COVERS
Westerns

★

GREEN COVERS
Non-Fiction

NON-FICTION TITLES
in the
Ulverscroft Large Print Series